THE ART
OF THE
EPIGRAPH

THE ART

OF THE

EPIGRAPH

HOW GREAT BOOKS BEGIN

Compiled and Edited by

ROSEMARY AHERN

ATRIA BOOKS

NEW YORK   LONDON   TORONTO   SYDNEY   NEW DELHI

ATRIA BOOKS
A Division of Simon & Schuster, Inc.
1230 Avenue of the Americas
New York, NY 10020

First Atria Books hardcover edition October 2012

ATRIA B O O K S and colophon are trademarks of Simon & Schuster, Inc.

For information about special discounts for bulk purchases, please contact Simon & Schuster Special Sales at 1-866-506-1949 or business@simonandschuster.com.

The Simon & Schuster Speakers Bureau can bring authors to your live event. For more information or to book an event, contact the Simon & Schuster Speakers Bureau at 1-866-248-3049 or visit our website at www.simonspeakers.com.

Designed by Kyoko Watanabe

Manufactured in the United States of America

10   9   8   7   6   5   4   3   2   1

Library of Congress Cataloging-in-Publication Data

The art of the epigraph : how great books begin / compiled and edited by Rosemary Ahern. — First Atria Books hardcover edition.
pp. cm.
1. Epigraphs (Literature). I. Ahern, Rosemary.
PN6081.A78 2012
808.88'2—dc23   2012020201

ISBN 978-1-4516-9324-9
ISBN 978-1-4516-9327-0 (ebook)

for ML

CONTENTS

For books continue each other in spite of our habit of judging them separately.

—VIRGINIA WOOLF

Off I go, rummaging about in books for sayings which please me.

—MICHEL DE MONTAIGNE

INTRODUCTION

I'm always surprised when someone claims not to read epigraphs. To me, that's an offering refused, a pleasure skipped. Those intriguing quotations, sayings, snippets of songs and poems, do more than just set the tone for the experience ahead: the epigraph informs us about the author's sensibility. Are we in the hands of a literalist or a wit? A cynic or a romantic? A writer of great ambition or a miniaturist? The epigraph hints at hidden stories and frequently comes with one of its own.

In hunting for epigraphs, I've discovered them as far back as the fourteenth century, in *The Canterbury Tales*, and I wouldn't be surprised if a more serious scholar traced the tradition back even further. The cumbersome (occasionally amusing) prefaces found in early novels like *Don Quixote* (1605) and *Gulliver's Travels* (1726) can be considered the literary forebears of the crisp, succinct epigrams that became the fashion in the twentieth century. Glamorous modernists like Hemingway and Fitzgerald popularized epigraphs, challenging authors to appear as learned and clever in their use of them ever since.

Some of my favorite authors are purists who present their work without outside association or adornment, without a wink or a clue. Flaubert, Edith Wharton, Virginia Woolf, Patti Smith. I respect and admire their silence before their books begin. However, this book celebrates the generosity of authors willing to part the curtain and show us a glimpse of their mental furniture; to give us a preview of what they think is vital, funny, and true. George Eliot, Vladimir Nabokov, C. S. Lewis, Lorrie Moore. Of course, their books would be every bit as memorable and important without epigraphs appended, but wouldn't we miss that extra element of anticipation? It would be like going to see *Vertigo* or *Midnight in Paris* and not taking your seat until after the opening title sequence. I always want to see how mood is established—and to submit.

Epigraphs appeal to those of us who occasionally need the kind of bolstering an ingenious turn of phrase or inspiring piece of wisdom can provide. I'm with Dorothy Parker when she says, "I might repeat to myself, slowly and soothingly, a list of quotations beautiful from minds profound—if I can remember any of the damn things." Thankfully, memory aides abound in the front matter of many of the world's best books. All that truth, humor, and novelty of expression presorted for us by consummate artists and cherished friends.

So yes, *The Art of the Epigraph* can be enjoyed like any quotation book. Here you will find advice on how to live well, be brave, avoid mistakes, apply the correct etiquette, adjust your expectations, appreciate quirkiness (your own and others'), attract a lover, break out of a rut, and dodge obligations. But you will also encounter fascinating conversations conducted over centuries and across cultures and genres. Writers communing with other writers, sometimes resulting in odd but delightful coincidences, like the fact that Susan Sontag and Mary Higgins Clark both turned to Tennyson when selecting epigraphs for their books. Divisions disappear; ideas and affinities are more clearly revealed.

Epigraphs remind us that writers are readers. I suppose that is what I like best about them. The experience I have when I read, encountering lines that perfectly express what I believe but can't articulate, that open up a new point of view, that make me feel understood or filled with joy, as brilliant and lofty as I might consider that book's author—it happens to them too. And that's what's on display in the epigraph: an author acknowledging his or her place in the fellowship of readers.

EDITOR'S NOTE

The *Oxford English Dictionary* defines "epigraph" as "the short quotation or motto placed at the commencement of a book, chapter, etc." In compiling *The Art of the Epigraph*, I have primarily chosen quotations that open the work in question. However, I have occasionally selected epigraphs from chapters or parts when doing so would allow classics like *The Red and the Black*, *Middlemarch,* and *The Souls of Black Folk* to be represented—or when an interior quote simply proved impossible to resist.

It should be noted that many authors adorn their opening pages with two, three, even several epigraphs. With a few exceptions, I have selected one quote from the crop. Some authors present their epigraphs unattributed. Where it has been possible to determine the source, I've annotated the entry to give that information. A few quotes, however, have managed to elude me. I've chosen to include a handful of epigraphs that originally appeared in Latin, French, or Italian without English translation. In *The Art of the Epigraph*, these quotes appear in their English translations only.

Translations aside, a conscious choice was made not to

standardize spelling, punctuation, styling, and other authorial idiosyncrasies that turn up in epigraphs. Except for variations in line breaks, epigraphs appear exactly as they do in the original editions of the books they were drawn from.

Finally, the publication dates listed herein represent the date of first publication in book form, be that in America or abroad.

THE ART

OF THE

EPIGRAPH

LIFE

One generation passeth away, and another generation cometh; but the earth abideth forever ...
The sun also ariseth, and the sun goeth down,
and hasteth to the place where he arose ... The
wind goeth toward the south, and turneth about
unto the north; it whirleth about continually,
and the wind returneth again according to his
circuits ... All the rivers run into the sea; yet the
sea is not full; unto the place from whence the
rivers come, thither they return again.

—ECCLESIASTES

In *The Sun Also Rises* (1926), Ernest Hemingway

Taking it slowly fixes everything.

—ENNIUS

In *The Red and the Black* (1830), Stendhal

One of the many pleasures of reading Stendhal is his liberal use of epigraphs, which offer wry commentary on the chapters they announce. The great translator Burton Raffel warns that Stendhal had a notorious habit of writing the epigraphs himself and ascribing them to elevated or otherwise unlikely sources. We could be skeptical, but why not play along? Hailed as the "Homer of Rome," Quintus Ennius (239–169 BC) was born in southern Italy, in what is today Calabria, where Greek was then the language of the upper classes. He learned Latin as a soldier in the Second Punic War and was taken to Rome by Cato the Elder. Working as a teacher and translator of Greek, Ennius began writing poetry, eventually producing the epic *Annales,* which recounted Rome's history from the fall of Troy to Ennius's own time. It was the most famous poem in the Roman world until Virgil's *Aeneid* supplanted it nearly three hundred years later.

Remember that the life of this world is but a sport and a pastime . . .

—KORAN, LVII 19

In *A Sport and a Pastime* (1967), James Salter

Somebody said lift that bale.

—RAY CHARLES SINGING "OL' MAN RIVER"

In *Beautiful Losers* (1966), Leonard Cohen

Life treads on life, and heart on heart;
We press too close in church and mart
To keep a dream of grave apart.

—MRS. BROWNING

In *The Souls of Black Folk* (1903), W. E. B. Du Bois

This epigraph opens the chapter "Of the Sons of Masters and Men," in which Du Bois meditates on the history of colonialism and race relations, concluding that "only by a union of intelligence and sympathy across the color-line . . . shall justice and right triumph." The quotation comes from "A Vision of the Poet" by Elizabeth Barrett Browning (1806–1861), who was outspoken in her opposition to slavery.

Some of it wasn't very nice, but most of it was beautiful.

—DOROTHY GALE, *THE WIZARD OF OZ*

In *Beautiful People* (2005), Simon Doonan

O my soul, do not aspire to immortal life, but exhaust the limits of the possible.

—PINDAR, *PYTHIAN* III

In *The Myth of Sisyphus* (1942), Albert Camus

Did I request thee, Maker, from my clay
To mold me Man, did I solicit thee
From darkness to promote me?—

—PARADISE LOST (X. 743–45)

In *Frankenstein* (1818), Mary Shelley

Mary Shelley was just nineteen when *Frankenstein* was published anonymously. Although the novel sold well, Shelley was too dogged by scandal and debts incurred by her husband, the poet Percy Bysshe Shelley, to receive any benefit from it. In fact, most people believed that Percy Shelley was the true author, doubting that a young girl could possess the kind of experience that would produce such a dark imagination. In fact, Shelley was well acquainted with death and the desire to resurrect life. Her mother, Mary Wollstonecraft, feminist and author of *A Vindication of the Rights of Women*, had died of an infection two weeks after giving birth to her. Mary herself had already suffered the death of one child before writing *Frankenstein*, and the child she was carrying while writing the novel would survive less than a year. A journal entry from 1815 reads: "Dream that my little baby came to life again; that it had only been cold, and that we rubbed it before the fire, and it lives."

February 19. Hopes?
February 20. Unnoticeable life. Noticeable
    failure.
February 25. A letter.

—FROM KAFKA'S DIARY, 1922

In *Running the Books: The Adventures of an Accidental Prison Librarian* (2010), Avi Steinberg

Nineteen twenty-two was not a good year for Kafka. Suffering from tuberculosis, his health declined to such a degree that he gave up writing fiction. He instructed his friend and literary executor, Max Brod, to burn all his manuscripts and papers after his death. Brod can be forgiven for not granting his friend's dying wish, as we wouldn't have *The Trial*, *The Castle*, or *Amerika* otherwise.

All the lives we could live, all the people we will never know, never will be, they are everywhere. That is what the world is.

—ALEKSANDAR HEMON,
THE LAZARUS PROJECT

In *Let the Great World Spin* (2009), Colum McCann

There is grandeur in this view of life, with its several powers, having been originally breathed into a few forms or into one; and that, whilst this planet has gone cycling on according to the fixed law of gravity, from so simple a beginning endless forms most beautiful and most wonderful have been, and are being evolved.

—CHARLES DARWIN, *ON THE ORIGIN OF SPECIES*

In *The Story of Edgar Sawtelle* (2008), David Wroblewski

The dirty nurse, Experience . . .

—TENNYSON

In *Regarding the Pain of Others* (2002), Susan Sontag

If we had a keen vision and feeling of all ordinary human life, it would be like hearing the grass grow and the squirrel's heart beat, and we should die of that roar which lies on the other side of silence.

—GEORGE ELIOT

In *Unless* (2002), Carol Shields

Traveling is a brutality. It forces you to trust strangers and to lose sight of all that familiar comfort of home and friends. You are constantly off balance. Nothing is yours except the essential things—air, sleep, dreams, the sun, the sky—all things tending toward the eternal or what we imagine of it.

—PAVESE

In *The Comfort of Strangers* (1981), Ian McEwan

Cesare Pavese (1908–1950), a towering figure in twentieth-century Italian cultural history, fell in love with American literature as a student in Turin. He wrote his thesis on Walt Whitman, and *Moby-Dick* was his favorite book. He began writing stories, poems, and novels, but his anti-Fascist activities landed him in one of Mussolini's prisons for three years. With his own work censored, Pavese began translating Herman Melville, Gertrude Stein, William Faulkner, Charles Dickens, and others, and it is through his translations that most Italian readers first encountered these authors. After the war, Pavese's novels *Before the Cock Crows*, *August Holiday*, and *Dialogues with Leucò* earned him great acclaim. Yet, at the height of his success, he committed suicide after a failed love affair. He was forty-one years old.

After all, my dear fellow, life, Anaxagoras has said, is a journey.

—BERGOTTE

In *The Dream Life of Balso Snell* (1931), Nathanael West

The journey was cut short for Nathanael West (1903–1940), who died at thirty-seven, his literary talents unrecognized. He had spectacular bad luck as an author: one of his publishers went bankrupt, and his darkly comic vision never caught on with Depression-era readers. Broke, West went to Hollywood to work as a screenwriter. There he fell in love with Eileen McKenney, heroine of her sister Ruth's popular book, *My Sister Eileen*. The couple was married less than a year when a car crash killed them both. This tragedy provoked interest in West and led to reissues of his novels and his posthumous fame. "Bergotte" is the author young Marcel worships in Proust's *In Search of Lost Time*; Anaxagoras was an influential Greek philosopher during the golden age of Pericles.

But there are two quite distinct things—given the wonderful place he's in—that may have happened to him. One is that he may have got brutalized. The other is that he may have got refined.

—HENRY JAMES, *THE AMBASSADORS*

In *Foreign Bodies* (2010), Cynthia Ozick

TELL THE TRUTH

Honesty's the best policy.

—MIGUEL DE CERVANTES

Liars prosper.

—ANONYMOUS

In *On Writing* (2000), Stephen King

Truth is the daughter of time.

—OLD PROVERB

In *The Daughter of Time* (1951), Josephine Tey

What stops a man who can laugh from speaking the truth?

—HORACE

In *Parliament of Whores* (1991), P. J. O'Rourke

By Woden, God of the Saxons,
From whence comes Wensday, that is
  Wodensday, Truth is a thing that ever
  I will keep
Unto thylke day which I creep into
My sepulchre—

—CARTWRIGHT

In "Rip Van Winkle," from *The Sketch Book of Geoffrey Crayon, Gent.* (1819), Washington Irving

One of the first American short stories was actually written in Birmingham, England, where Irving had gone after the War of 1812 to help salvage his family's business interests. The epigraph is from a seventeenth-century play, *The Ordinary*, by William Cartwright (1611–1643), member of the Sons of Ben, a group of playwrights heavily influenced by Ben Jonson.

Fairy tales are more than true: not because they tell us that dragons exist, but because they tell us that dragons can be beaten.

—G. K. CHESTERTON

In *Coraline* (2002), Neil Gaiman

Although widely viewed as a Catholic reactionary, Chesterton is credited with inspiring Mohandas Gandhi to take up the fight for Indian independence from British rule. A column Chesterton wrote in 1909 so impressed Gandhi that he translated it into Gujarati and then proceeded to write his own book addressing the problems of colonialism and how to achieve reform through civil disobedience.

What is truth, said jesting Pilate, and did not stay for an answer.

—FRANCIS BACON, CIRCA 1600

In *You'll Never Eat Lunch in This Town Again* (1991), Julia Phillips

You know the best you can expect is to avoid the worst.

—ITALO CALVINO, *IF ON A WINTER'S NIGHT A TRAVELER*

In *If the River Was Whiskey* (1989), T. Coraghessan Boyle

They're nice to have. A dog.
— F. SCOTT FITZGERALD, *THE GREAT GATSBY*

In *Straight Man* (1997), Richard Russo

Russo's novel opens with a prologue in which his middle-aged protagonist is a young boy who relentlessly begs his parents for a dog, only to be presented with an elderly Irish setter that promptly drops dead. As an adult, Hank Devereaux eventually gets a dog he names after Occam's razor, a theory (the simplest course of action is usually the right one) that he attempts to apply to the baffling complexities of midlife.

Tell the truth, tell the truth, tell the truth.

—SHERYL LOUISE MOLLER

In *Eat, Pray, Love* (2006), Elizabeth Gilbert

Perhaps it's not surprising, given Gilbert's title, that the epigraph comes from a nutritional therapist. Outside the pages of her memoir, Gilbert praises Moller for helping her get "to my place of perfect health. (And frankly, she got me to my place of perfect pants size as well.)"

They love truth when it reveals itself, and they hate it when it reveals themselves.

—SAINT AUGUSTINE

In *The Vivisector* (1970), Patrick White

Do not play this piece fast
It is never right to play Ragtime fast. . . .

—SCOTT JOPLIN

In *Ragtime* (1975), E. L. Doctorow

> There is no street with mute stones and no house without echoes.
>
> —GÓNGORA

In *Mystic River* (2001), Dennis Lehane

Luis de Góngora y Argote (1561–1627) was a Spanish Baroque poet and a contemporary of Cervantes, who admired Góngora's work, and Velázquez, who painted his portrait.

It is a profound and necessary truth that the deep things in science are not found because they are useful; they are found because it is possible to find them.

—ROBERT OPPENHEIMER

In *The Making of the Atomic Bomb* (1986), Richard Rhodes

What a strange power there is in clothing.

—ISAAC BASHEVIS SINGER

In *A Vintage Affair* (2009), Isabel Wolff

Oranges are not the only fruit.

—NELL GWYN

In *Oranges Are Not the Only Fruit* (1985),
Jeanette Winterson

Nell Gwyn (1650–1687) was a Restoration-era celebrity who began her career as a scantily dressed "orange girl," selling oranges and sweets to theater crowds and ferrying messages between men in the audience and the actresses backstage. King Charles II had recently made it legal for women to act in plays (prior to this female parts had been played by boys), and by age fifteen "pretty, witty Nell" was receiving glowing reviews for her performances. She was as famous for her lovers as for the parts she played, but her singular devotion to Charles II and her salty, down-to-earth manner earned her the public's undying affection.

Work without hope draws nectar in a sieve,
And hope without object cannot live.

—COLERIDGE

In *Nectar in a Sieve* (1954), Kamala Markandaya

A pioneering figure for Indians writing in English, Kamala Markandaya (1924–2004) also introduced Western readers to life in impoverished rural India in her international best seller, *Nectar in a Sieve*. Written less than a decade after India won independence from Britain, the novel portrays the lingering effects of colonialism and India's struggles with modernity.

In accumulating property for ourselves or our posterity, in founding a family or state, or acquiring fame even, we are mortal; but in dealing with the truth we are immortal, and need fear no change or accident.

—HENRY DAVID THOREAU

In *Lucky Man* (2002), Michael J. Fox

Every emancipation is a restoration of the human world and of human relationships to man himself.

—MARX, *ZUR JUDENFRAGE* (1844)

In *The French Lieutenant's Woman* (1969), John Fowles

Man knows no Master save creating Heaven,
Or those whom Choice and common Good
    ordain.

—THOMSON

In *Common Sense* (1776), Thomas Paine

Thomas Paine had tried his hand at being a corset maker, sailor, teacher, Methodist preacher, tax collector, and grocer before being introduced to Benjamin Franklin in London through an astronomer friend. Franklin convinced the bankrupt Paine that he could make a better life for himself in America. It didn't take him long. Less than two years after arriving in Philadelphia, Paine published the most brilliant and incendiary pamphlet of the American Revolution. The forty-eight-page pamphlet sold out instantly and began being printed throughout the colonies and Europe. Paine signed his royalties over to George Washington's Continental Army. The epigraph is taken from a 1736 poem, "Liberty," by James Thomson.

LOVE

Only connect . . .

In *Howards End* (1910), E. M. Forster

One of the most famous phrases in English literature occurs when a sensitive woman decides to marry an obtuse man. "I am not a fellow who bothers about my own inside," boasts businessman Henry Wilcox. Margaret Schlegel, his bohemian fiancée, is touchingly optimistic about the prospect of introducing Henry to the latent potential of his soul. "Only connect! That was the whole of her sermon. Only connect the prose and the passion, and both will be exalted, and human love will be seen at its height."

. . . Poor wounded name! My bosom as a bed
Shall lodge thee.

—W. SHAKESPEARE

In *Tess of the d'Urbervilles* (1891), Thomas Hardy

———————

To imagine that a person who intrigues us has
access to a way of life unknown and all the
more attractive for its mystery, to believe that
we will begin to live only through the love of
that person—what else is this but the birth of
great passion?

—MARCEL PROUST, FROM THE
MISTRANSLATION OF Y. K. KARAOSMANOĞLU

In *The White Castle* (1985), Orhan Pamuk

Then wear the gold hat, if that will move her;
    If you can bounce high, bounce for her
        too,
Till she cry "lover, gold-hatted, high-bouncing
    lover,
    I must have you!"

—THOMAS PARKE D'INVILLIERS

In *The Great Gatsby* (1925), F. Scott Fitzgerald

Fitzgerald's epigraph and its source are entirely fictitious. D'Invilliers is a character from Fitzgerald's first novel, *This Side of Paradise*, a classmate of protagonist Amory Blaine and the one who introduces Blaine to the joys of poetry. *Gold-hatted Gatsby* was one of Fitzgerald's original titles for the novel; thankfully, wiser heads prevailed.

Love is nothing, nothing, nothing like they say.
—LIZ PHAIR

In *Good in Bed* (2001), Jennifer Weiner

O love is the crooked thing . . .
—W. B. YEATS, "BROWN PENNY"

In *The Love Letter* (1995), Cathleen Schine

People would never fall in love if they hadn't heard love talked about.

—FRANÇOIS DE LA ROCHEFOUCAULD

In *The Marriage Plot* (2011), Jeffrey Eugenides

The postmodern quality of this quote perfectly suits Eugenides's story of a trio of college students studying semiotics and falling in love anyway. But it was written three hundred years before Roland Barthes was born. La Rochefoucauld was a seventeenth-century nobleman whose literary reputation rests on his *Maximes* (1665), a collection of over 500 "gently cynical" epigrams whose clarity and insight remain fresh 350 years after they were first set down on paper.

I am accustoming myself to the idea of regarding every sexual act as a process in which four persons are involved. We shall have a lot to discuss about that.

—S. FREUD: LETTERS

In *Justine* (1957), Lawrence Durrell

Rage, love's color,
love, the color of oblivion.

—LUIS CERNUDA

In *Poet in New York* (1940), Federico García Lorca

Alas! When passion is both meek and wild!

—JOHN KEATS

In *Revolutionary Road* (1961), Richard Yates

What better description of suburban life? Yates found the perfect evocation for his classic novel of the desolation and thwarted passions of the American suburb in the unlikeliest of sources: Keats's 1820 epic poem "Isabella; or, The Pot of Basil," which depicts a bloody Renaissance tragedy.

SPEAKER: Stranger, what do you seek or ask from us?

TAMINO: Friendship and love.

SPEAKER: And are you prepared even if it costs you your life?

TAMINO: I am.

—*THE MAGIC FLUTE*,
WOLFGANG AMADEUS MOZART

In *Bel Canto* (2001), Ann Patchett

His heart is a suspended lute;
Whenever one touches it, it resounds.

—BÉRANGER

In "The Fall of the House of Usher" (1839),
Edgar Allan Poe

Pierre-Jean de Béranger (1780–1857) was the most famous *chansonnier* (songwriter) of his day. His leftist politics made him immensely popular—and also landed him in prison. His songs are credited with helping bring about the Revolution of 1830. Although he eventually became a favorite of the king, and was showered with appointments and favors, Béranger refused them all. He asked only for a pension for his friend Rouget de Lisle, author of the "Marseillaise," who was elderly and living in poverty.

Love is what happens between two lovers.

—ROGER VAILLAND

In *A Certain Smile* (1956), Françoise Sagan

———————

Assuming that our energies are sufficient, love is interminable.

—JIM HARRISON, *THE ROAD HOME*

In *Three Junes* (2002), Julia Glass

The words I am about to express:
They now have their own crowned goddess.

—LEANDRO DÍAZ

In *Love in the Time of Cholera* (1988), Gabriel García
Márquez

García Márquez's epigraph is drawn from the lyrics of "La
diosa coronada" by Leandro José Díaz Duarte (born 1928).
Born blind, Díaz nonetheless became one of the most famous singer songwriters of the "Vallenato" tradition, a type
of folk music from the northern coast of Colombia. "I think
God didn't put eyes in my face because he took his time to
put eyes in my soul," Díaz has said, sounding like one of
García Márquez's characters.

THE RIVER OF TIME

... A story that was the subject of every variety of misrepresentation, not only by those who then lived but likewise in succeeding times: so true is it that all transactions of preeminent importance are wrapt in doubt and obscurity; while some hold for certain facts the most precarious hearsays, others turn facts into falsehood; and both are exaggerated by posterity.

—TACITUS

In *I, Claudius* (1934), Robert Graves

The best days . . . are the first to flee—

—VIRGIL

In *My Ántonia* (1918), Willa Cather

What web is this
    Of will be, is, and was?

—JORGE LUIS BORGES

In *Passages* (1976), Gail Sheehy

There is no present or future—only the past, happening over and over again—now.
—EUGENE O'NEILL, *A MOON FOR THE MISBEGOTTEN*

In *Trinity* (1976), Leon Uris

————————◆————————

The distinction between past, present and future is an illusion, but a very persistent one.
—ALBERT EINSTEIN

In *The Map of Time* (2011), Félix J. Palma

> Clock time is our bank manager, tax collector, police inspector; this inner time is our wife.
>
> —J. B. PRIESTLEY

In *The Time Traveler's Wife* (2003), Audrey Niffenegger

Novelist, essayist, and playwright J. B. Priestley (1894–1984) was obsessed by time. Influenced by a scientific treatise, *An Experiment with Time*, written in 1927 by Irish engineer J. W. Dunne, Priestley came to believe that we exist in multiple temporal dimensions—chronological time being just one of those dimensions and not the one where our true nature dwells. He wrote a series of "Time Plays" in the 1930s and '40s exploring alternative theories of time, including the very popular *An Inspector Calls*.

Time we may comprehend, 'tis but five days
elder than ourselves.

—SIR THOMAS BROWNE,
RELIGIO MEDICI, 1642

In *Time's Arrow, Time's Cycle* (1987), Stephen Jay Gould

Physician and philosopher, Browne was a seventeenth-
century polymath whose interests included theology,
medicine, botany, and alchemy. He was also an avid book
collector, amassing one of the most extensive private librar-
ies in Europe. In 1711, twenty-nine years after Browne's
death, more than 1,500 titles in eight languages went up for
auction. Jonathan Swift attended, and numerous titles sold
would form the foundation of the future British Library.

And I can see no reason why anyone should suppose that in the future the same motifs already heard will not be sounding still . . . put to use by reasonable men to reasonable ends, or by madmen to nonsense and disaster.

—JOSEPH CAMPBELL,
FOREWORD TO *THE MASKS OF GOD:
PRIMITIVE MYTHOLOGY*, 1969

In *The March of Folly* (1984), Barbara W. Tuchman

What is past is prologue

—INSCRIPTION IN
WASHINGTON, D.C., MUSEUM

In *White Teeth* (2000), Zadie Smith

Of old the Hellenic race was marked off from the barbarian as more keen-witted and more free from nonsense.

—HERODOTUS I:60

In *Mythology* (1942), Edith Hamilton

The headmistress of Bryn Mawr Preparatory school for twenty-six years, Edith Hamilton (1867–1963) did not start her writing career until after she retired. She was seventy-five when *Mythology* was published; the book remains one of the most commonly used texts in high school and college classes. Jackie Kennedy was a fan of Hamilton's work, and when President Kennedy was assassinated, she gave a copy of Hamilton's *The Greek Way* to his brother Robert, who said he took great comfort in the Hellenic creed of "in agony, learn wisdom."

I think one remains the same person through-out, merely passing, as it were, in these lapses of time from one room to another, but all in the same house.

—J. M. BARRIE

In *Manhattan, When I Was Young* (1995), Mary Cantwell

Cantwell takes these lines from the ten-page dedication, addressed to "The Five," in the first printed edition of J. M. Barrie's play *Peter Pan; or, The Boy Who Wouldn't Grow Up*. "The Five" are the five sons of Arthur and Sylvia Llewelyn Davies, who served as inspiration for Peter and the "lost boys." Barrie would eventually adopt the five boys after their parents' deaths. "I made Peter by rubbing the five of you violently together, as savages with two sticks produce a flame. That is all he is, the spark I got from you," he writes. Although *Peter Pan* was first performed in 1904, it was not published until 1928, by which time George Llewelyn Davies had been killed in action in World War I and his brother Michael had died in a drowning accident.

Human Folly

"How did you go bankrupt?" Bill asked.

"Two ways," Mike said. "Gradually and then suddenly."

—*THE SUN ALSO RISES*

In *Bright Lights, Big City* (1984), Jay McInerney

It is certain my Conviction gains infinitely, the moment another soul will believe in it.

—NOVALIS

In *Lord Jim* (1900), Joseph Conrad

Men play at tragedy because they do not believe in the reality of the tragedy which is actually being staged in the civilised world.

—JOSÉ ORTEGA Y GASSET

In *Into Thin Air* (1997), Jon Krakauer

> More tears are shed over answered prayers than
> unanswered ones.
>
> —SAINT TERESA

In *Answered Prayers* (1987), Truman Capote

More than tears were shed over *Answered Prayers*. Capote's
gossipy novel cost him many friendships, as well as his
privileged place in New York's high society. He had put the
lives and secrets of his "swans"—socialites like Babe Paley,
Slim Keith, and Gloria Vanderbilt—on public display, and
none would ever speak to him again. The title of the book,
as well as its epigraph, comes from Saint Teresa of Ávila
(1515–1582), a Spanish mystic whose spiritual autobiography, *The Interior Castle*, is considered by many to be
the equal of Saint Augustine's *Confessions*. Charming and
extroverted, Sister Teresa was far from the stereotype of a
dour, ascetic nun. She would have been right at home on a
banquette at La Côte Basque. When criticized for enjoying
a fine meal, Teresa said, "There's a time for partridge and a
time for penance."

If his inmost heart could have been laid open there would have been discovered that dream of undying fame; which, dream as it is, is more powerful than a thousand realities.

—NATHANIEL HAWTHORNE, *FANSHAWE*

In *A Fan's Notes* (1968), Frederick Exley

To a man with a hammer, everything looks like a nail.

—MARK TWAIN

In *Zeitoun* (2009), Dave Eggers

The treasure which you think not worth taking trouble and pains to find, this one alone is the real treasure you are longing for all your life. The glittering treasure you are hunting for day and night lies buried on the other side of that hill yonder.

In *The Treasure of the Sierra Madre* (1927), B. Traven

B. Traven is possibly the most mysterious author of all time. The place and date of his birth are unknown. There are numerous theories as to the true identity of this author, who spent his productive years in Mexico, wrote his novels in German, but seemed to have intimate knowledge of Chicago and other American locales. Was he the illegitimate son of Kaiser Wilhelm II, as one such theory holds? When his widow eventually came forward more than twenty years after his death, she claimed Traven was Ret Marut, a German actor turned anarchist-revolutionary who had been imprisoned and sentenced to death in the years after World War I. On the way to being executed, he escaped German authorities and always feared extradition, living "something like ten lives" in order to cover his tracks.

The devil . . . prowde spirite . . . cannot endure
to be mocked.

—THOMAS MORE

In *The Screwtape Letters* (1942), C. S. Lewis

What would this Man? Now, upward will he
    soar,
        And little less than angel, would be more;
Now looking downwards, just as grieved
    appears
        To want the strength of bulls, the fur
        of bears.

—ALEXANDER POPE

In *Less Than Angels* (1955), Barbara Pym

There go the ships; there is that Leviathan whom thou hast made to play therein.

—PSALMS

Very like a whale.

—HAMLET

Ten or fifteen gallons of blood are thrown out of the heart at a stroke, with immense velocity.

—JOHN HUNTER'S ACCOUNT OF
THE DISSECTION OF A WHALE
(A SMALL SIZED ONE.)

So be cheery, my lads, let your hearts never fail,
While the bold harpooner is striking the
    whale!

—NANTUCKET SONG

In *Moby-Dick* (1851), Herman Melville

While many authors preface their works with two or more epigraphs, Melville takes the prize by including nearly eighty in *Moby-Dick*. Melville sees his "extracts" as "affording a glancing bird's eye view of what has been promiscuously said, thought, fancied, and sung of Leviathan, by many nations and generations." While the catalog of whale references is fascinating and entertaining, Melville admonishes us not to take the assembled quotations as "veritable gospel cetology."

Blessed are the undefiled.

In *The Good Soldier* (1915), Ford Madox Ford

Ford's unattributed epigraph comes from Psalm 119.

The most difficult subjects can be explained to the most slow-witted man if he has not formed any idea of them already; but the simplest thing cannot be made clear to the most intelligent man if he is firmly persuaded that he knows already, without a shadow of a doubt, what is laid before him.

—LEO TOLSTOY, 1897

In *The Big Short* (2010), Michael Lewis

And they went to sea in a Sieve.

—EDWARD LEAR

In *The Yiddish Policemen's Union* (2007), Michael Chabon

Chabon's epigraph is taken from a delightful poem entitled "The Jumblies," written by the same man who penned "The Owl and the Pussy Cat." Edward Lear (1812–1888) was an itinerant landscape painter before becoming successful as the author of popular nonsense verse. He suffered from depression (which he referred to as "the morbids") and epilepsy, which led to periods of self-imposed isolation. He nonetheless managed to form lasting friendships with Tennyson, the Pre-Raphaelite painter William Holman Hunt, and other Victorian notables.

The heart, to be sure, always has something to say about what is to come, to him who heeds it. But what does the heart know? Only a little of what has already happened.

—*I PROMESSI SPOSI*, CHAPTER VIII

In *The Garden of the Finzi-Continis* (1962),
Giorgio Bassani

I Promessi sposi (*The Betrothed*) by Alessandro Manzoni is considered the greatest Italian novel of all time. Published in 1827, it was translated into English by Edgar Allan Poe. Manzoni's advocacy of a united Italy made him a hero of the Risorgimento, the nationalist movement to free the country from Austrian and other foreign control. Manzoni's death at age eighty-eight was an occasion for national mourning; Verdi composed his "Manzoni" requiem in homage.

I am pessimistic about the human race because it is too ingenious for its own good. Our approach to nature is to beat it into submission. We would stand a better chance of survival if we accommodated ourselves to this planet and viewed it appreciatively instead of skeptically and dictatorially.

—E. B. WHITE

In *Silent Spring* (1962), Rachel Carson

You are all a lost generation.

—GERTRUDE STEIN, in conversation

In *The Sun Also Rises* (1926), Ernest Hemingway

Hemingway would later report that the "lost generation" label did not originate with Stein. She borrowed the concept and phrase from the owner of the garage where she brought her old Model T Ford for repair. When a young mechanic's skills were not up to Stein's ignition trouble, the World War I veteran was berated by the garage owner who shouted: "You are all a *génération perdue.*" Stein used the term for her coterie of literary young men who had drifted to Paris in the postwar years more affectionately, but Hemingway came to regret publicizing the remark. He called it a piece of "splendid bombast" in a letter to Maxwell Perkins, his editor.

FOLLOW YOUR BLISS

Surprised by joy—impatient as the wind.

—WORDSWORTH

In *Surprised by Joy* (1955), C. S. Lewis

Although this autobiography recounting Lewis's embrace of Christianity as a young professor at Oxford in the 1930s is completely unrelated to his late-in-life marriage to Joy Gresham, an American poet seventeen years his junior, his friends couldn't resist teasing that Lewis really had been "surprised by Joy."

Ah cannot wee,
As well as cocks and lyons jocund be,
After such pleasures?

—JOHN DONNE

In *After Such Pleasures* (1933), Dorothy Parker

Although best known for pious works like "Death Be Not Proud" and "No Man Is an Island," John Donne (1572–1631) had a subversive wit and unsentimental vision of love and romance that rival Dorothy Parker's. (He once summed up his marriage "John Donne. Anne Donne. Undone.") Donne's work fell out of favor almost immediately after his death, but, thanks to T. S. Eliot and Ezra Pound, interest was revived in the 1920s. Here's hoping he proved prescient when he said: "Death is an ascension to a better library."

The senses, rebellious and ignorant lords

In *The Pure and the Impure* (1932), Colette

Appropriately, the great French writer Colette (1873–1954) began writing her journalistic treatise on sensual pleasure and the ways in which our lives are driven, shaped, and destroyed by desire while cruising the Norwegian fjords on a yacht named *Eros*. Generations of critics and readers have struggled with this strange, difficult work, but Colette believed it to be her best book and pronounced it her favorite.

There are seductions that should be in the Smithsonian Institute, right next to *The Spirit of St. Louis*.

In *Trout Fishing in America* (1967), Richard Brautigan

An unknown poet from San Francisco's Haight-Ashbury district, Brautigan became the "voice of the 1960s counterculture" when his first novel, *Trout Fishing in America*, sold over two million copies. Subsequent decades were less kind. He would commit suicide in 1984 after a lifelong battle with depression. Brautigan's friend, the writer Thomas McGuane, said, "When the 1960s ended, he was the baby thrown out with the bathwater."

We have shared out like thieves the amazing treasure of nights and days

—J. L. BORGES

In *The Mysteries of Pittsburgh* (1988), Michael Chabon

For some years I have been afflicted with the belief that Flight is possible to man.

—WILBUR WRIGHT, LETTER, MAY 13, 1900

In *The Spirit of the Place* (2008), Samuel Shem

The gloom of the world is but a shadow; behind it, yet within our reach, is joy. Take joy.

—FRA GIOVANNI GIOCONDO

In *Slow Love* (2010), Dominique Browning

Fra Giocando was a fifteenth-century Franciscan priest and renowned Renaissance architect. He designed a palace for Holy Roman emperor Maximilian I and brought the architectural ideas and styles of the Italian Renaissance to France, where he served as "royal architect" between 1496 and 1499. At the end of his life, he supervised the construction of Saint Peter's Basilica in Rome along with the painter Raphael and the sculptor and engineer Giuliano di Sangallo.

COURAGE

Sometimes when the fights begin,
I think I'll let the dragons win,
But then again, perhaps I won't,
Because they're dragons, and I don't.

—A. A. MILNE

In *Coming of Age* (1995), Studs Terkel

He well knows what snares are spread about his path, from personal animosity . . . and possibly from popular delusion. But he has put to hazard his ease, his security, his interest, his power, even his . . . popularity. . . . He is traduced and abused for his supposed motives. He will remember that obloquy is a necessary ingredient in the composition of all true glory: he will remember . . . that calumny and abuse are essential parts of triumph . . . He may live long, he may do much. But here is the summit. He never can exceed what he does this day.

—EDMUND BURKE's eulogy of Charles
James Fox for his attack upon the tyranny
of the East India Company—House
of Commons, December 1, 1783

In *Profiles in Courage* (1956), John F. Kennedy

In 1954, then-senator Kennedy took a leave of absence to recover from back surgery and began researching and writing the book that would become *Profiles in Courage*. Kennedy drafted much of the book longhand, but relied heavily on Theodore Sorensen, a speechwriter and close aide whom he referred to as "my intellectual blood bank." (Sorensen would later become President Kennedy's White House counsel.) The book received the Pulitzer Prize for History in 1957.

Some men see things the way they are, and say why, I dream of things that never were, and say why not."

In *Shoeless Joe* (1982), W. P. Kinsella

Give me silence, water, hope
Give me struggle, iron, volcanoes

—NERUDA

In *Desert Solitaire* (1968), Edward Abbey

And he sets his mind to unknown arts.

—OVID, *METAMORPHOSES*, VIII, 188.

In *A Portrait of the Artist as a Young Man* (1916), James Joyce

Ovid is speaking of the architect and inventor Daedalus, a figure from Greek mythology, in the line Joyce selects as the epigraph to his first novel (whose hero he names Stephen Dedalus). "Unknown arts" refers to human flight. Imprisoned on the isle of Crete, Daedalus engineers his escape by fashioning wings out of feathers and beeswax for himself and his son, Icarus, who flies too close to the sun, thus melting his wings and plunging to his death. In 1895, an Irishman, Trinity College professor George Francis FitzGerald, attempted to replicate Daedalus's feat, but only managed to attain an altitude of six inches on the bat-like wings he had constructed. The critic Hugh Kenner has speculated that a thirteen-year-old Joyce may have been among the crowd who witnessed this less-than-historic flight.

To conclude, therefore, let no man out of a weak conceit of sobriety, or an ill-tempered moderation, think or maintain, that a man can search too far or be too well studied in the book of God's word, or in the book of God's works; divinity or philosophy; but rather let men endeavour an endless progress or proficience in both.

—BACON, *ADVANCEMENT OF LEARNING*

In *On the Origin of Species* (1859), Charles Darwin

Darwin had his theory of natural selection worked out by 1838, yet it took him twenty years to publish it. Fear of persecution by religious authorities may have been a factor in the delay. *Origin*'s epigraph both anticipates and cleverly deflects charges of heresy. Although controversy could not be avoided, it turned *On the Origin of Species* into an instant best seller and guaranteed its place in the literary and scientific canon.

A mind that is stretched to a new idea never returns to its original dimension.

—OLIVER WENDELL HOLMES

In *A Natural History of the Senses* (1990), Diane Ackerman

That is at bottom the only courage that is demanded of us: to have courage for the most strange, the most singular and the most inexplicable that we may encounter. That mankind has in this sense been cowardly has done life endless harm; the experiences that are called "visions," the whole so-called "spirit-world," death, all those things that are so closely akin to us, have by daily parrying been so crowded out of life that the senses with which we could have grasped them are atrophied. To say nothing of God."

—RAINER MARIA RILKE

In *The Snow Leopard* (1978), Peter Matthiessen

Leap before you look.

—OLD SLAVONIC MAXIM

In *Travels with Myself and Another* (1978), Martha Gellhorn

"Leap before you look" is exactly what Gellhorn did in marrying Ernest Hemingway, the "Another" in the title of the celebrated novelist and war correspondent's only autobiography. Gellhorn describes a reporting trip to the Far East—the couple's "honeymoon"—referring to Hemingway as "UC" (Unwilling Companion). It wasn't long before Hemingway's rages and controlling behavior made Gellhorn the UC and she left him.

And now (Theseus drawing nigh his) native land
in laurelled car after battling with the Scithian
folk, etc.

—STATIUS

In *The Canterbury Tales* (circa 1476), Geoffrey Chaucer

This epigraph precedes "The Knight's Tale" and is taken
from the *Thebaid* of first-century Roman poet Publius Pa-
pinius Statius. Chaucer wrote *The Canterbury Tales* in the
late 1300s, before the printing press had been invented. Although fairly widely circulated in manuscript form, it would
be one hundred years before William Caxton printed the
first edition of *The Canterbury Tales*. Caxton is believed to
have introduced the printing press to England and to have
been the nation's first printer.

WARNINGS AND
LAMENTATIONS

"You are saved," cried Captain Delano, more and more astonished and pained; "you are saved: what has cast such a shadow upon you?"

—HERMAN MELVILLE, *BENITO CERENO*

In *Invisible Man* (1952), Ralph Ellison

I myself once saw, with my own eyes, the Sybil of Cumae hanging in a cage; and when the boys asked her "What wouldst thou prophesy, Sibyl?" she replied, "I want to die."

In "The Waste Land" (1922), T. S. Eliot

Perhaps the single most influential poem of the twentieth century, "The Waste Land" challenges readers with obscure references and numerous allusions to classical literature and mythology; parts of the poem are even written in Sanskrit. Eliot's epigraph is taken from the *Satyricon*, written circa AD 61 by Gaius Petronius, an adviser to the Roman emperor Nero. The Sibyl of Cumae was a prophetess so beautiful, the god Apollo promised her anything if she would spend a single night with him. The Sibyl asked for as many years of life as grains of sand she could hold in her hand. Apollo granted her wish; she reneged on the deal, and was thus cursed with eternal life without eternal youth. Over the centuries, she eventually shriveled to the size of a cricket.

Things look pretty bad right now
                    —MAJ. GEN. BRIGGS, AT SHILOH

In *Is Sex Necessary?* (1929), James Thurber and
E. B. White

Them that die'll be the lucky ones.
                    —LONG JOHN SILVER, *TREASURE ISLAND*

In *Please Kill Me: The Uncensored Oral History of Punk*
(1996), Legs McNeil and Gillian McCain

. . . small official notices had been just put up about the town, though in places where they would not attract much attention. It was hard to find in these notices any indication that the authorities were facing the situation squarely. The measures enjoined were far from Draconian and one had the feeling that many concessions had been made to a desire not to alarm the public.

—ALBERT CAMUS, *THE PLAGUE*

In *And the Band Played On* (1987), Randy Shilts

The first openly gay reporter for a major American newspaper, Shilts traced the history of the AIDS epidemic in *And the Band Played On*, documenting the failure of both the medical community and society at large to respond to the crisis. Historian Garry Wills wrote: "This book will be to gay liberation what Betty Friedan was to early feminism and Rachel Carson's *Silent Spring* was to environmentalism."

Two households both alike in dignity,
From ancient grudge break to new mutiny.

—ROMEO AND JULIET

In *The Forsyte Saga* (1922), John Galsworthy

Fairy Godmother, where were you when I needed you?

—CINDERELLA

In *What Color Is Your Parachute? A Practical Manual for Job-Hunters and Career-Changers* (1981 edition), Richard Nelson Bolles

"What war?" said the Prime Minister sharply. "No one has said anything to me about a war. I really think I should have been told. . . ."

And presently, like a circling typhoon, the sounds of battle began to return.

—EVELYN WAUGH, *VILE BODIES*

In *Speedboat* (1976), Renata Adler

And if the Babe is born a Boy
He's given to a Woman Old,
Who nails him down upon a rock,
Catches his shrieks in cups of gold.

—WILLIAM BLAKE

In *Grendel* (1971), John Gardner

> Man, man, one cannot live quite without pity.
> —DOSTOEVSKY: *CRIME AND PUNISHMENT*

In *Darkness at Noon* (1940), Arthur Koestler

At various points a Zionist, a Communist, and an anti-fascist, Koestler (1905–1983) led an eventful and controversial life. Covering the Spanish Civil War as a journalist for a British newspaper, Koestler was arrested by Franco's Nationalist forces, imprisoned, and sentenced to death. Following high-level negotiations, he was released after ninety-four days in captivity. This experience, along with his disgust at the show trials in Stalin's Russia, became the basis of *Darkness at Noon*. Koestler would be in prison again, this time in German-occupied France, when the book was published. In later years, he was a self-described "Casanova of causes" and counted George Orwell and Timothy Leary among his friends.

This is the patent age of new inventions
     For killing bodies, and for saving souls,
All propagated with the best intentions.

                         —BYRON

In *The Quiet American* (1955), Graham Greene

I accused her as though her prayers had really
worked the change: What did I do to you that
you had to condemn me to life?

     —GRAHAM GREENE, *THE END OF THE AFFAIR*

In *Angels* (1983), Denis Johnson

Great wits are sure to madness near allied
And thin partitions do their bounds divide.

—JOHN DRYDEN

In *Art and Madness: A Memoir of Lust Without Reason*
(2011), Anne Roiphe

The nobility has honesty painted in its eyes

—*DON GIOVANNI*, MOZART

In *A Noble Radiance* (1998), Donna Leon

I've seen the devil of violence and the devil of greed and the devil of hot desire; but, by all the stars! these were strong, lusty, red-eyed devils that swayed and drove men—men, I tell you. But as I stood on that hillside, I foresaw that in the blinding sunshine of that land, I would become acquainted with a flabby, pretending weak-eyed devil of rapacious and pitiless folly.

—CONRAD, *HEART OF DARKNESS*

In *Dog Soldiers* (1974), Robert Stone

The cattle are lowing,
The Baby awakes.
But the little Lord Jesus
No crying He makes

In *Slaughterhouse-Five* (1969), Kurt Vonnegut

Vonnegut's epigraph is taken from the Christmas carol "Away in a Manger." Tradition long held that the lyrics were written by none other than Protestant reformer Martin Luther (1483–1546). Vonnegut uses this sweet rhyme to make oblique and ominous reference to the firebombing of Dresden in World War II, the central episode in *Slaughterhouse-Five*, in which more than 100,000 people—including countless innocent children—were incinerated while they slept.

OFF THE MAP

If you are lucky enough to have lived in Paris as a young man, then wherever you go for the rest of your life, it stays with you, for Paris is a moveable feast.

—ERNEST HEMINGWAY to a friend, 1950

In *A Moveable Feast* (1964), Ernest Hemingway

I speak of Africa and golden joys.
—*HENRY IV*, ACT V, SC. 3 (SHAKESPEARE)

In *West with the Night* (1942), Beryl Markham

Beryl Markham (1902–1986) spent most of her life in British East Africa. She was one of the first women to hold a commercial pilot's license and, in 1936, became the first person to fly solo across the Atlantic from East to West. The title of her subsequent memoir makes reference to the fact that, unlike Charles Lindbergh and Amelia Earhart, she made her twenty-one-hour Atlantic crossing flying mostly in the dark. The famously egotistical Hemingway said he was "completely ashamed" of his own work after reading *West with the Night*. Rumors circulated for years that the book was actually written by Markham's third husband, Raoul Schumacher, a screenwriter and journalist. Markham's biographers have debated both sides of the authorship question, with no definitive resolution.

It's an odd thing, but anyone who disappears is said to be seen in San Francisco.

—OSCAR WILDE

In *Tales of the City* (1978), Armistead Maupin

where dreams and retail collide

—NIKE AD

In *The Mighty Walzer* (1999), Howard Jacobson

A New Yorker doesn't have to discover New York. He knows it's there all the time.

—WHITEY BIMSTEIN

In *Back Where I Came From* (1938), A. J. Liebling

Morris "Whitey" Bimstein (1897–1969) was a boxing legend. As a trainer and "cutman," he worked with twenty-five world boxing champions, including Jack Dempsey, Gene Tunney, Jake LaMotta, and Rocky Marciano. Bimstein grew up on the Lower East Side of Manhattan, and as an adult lived in the Bronx, but he could usually be found at Stillman's Gym on Eighth Avenue between Fifty-fourth and Fifty-fifth Streets. A. J. Liebling joined the staff of *The New Yorker* in 1935 and carried on a very public love affair with the city and its colorful characters in his "Wayward Press" columns.

Nothing can astound an American.

—JULES VERNE

In *Moon Palace* (1989), Paul Auster

There are certain sections of New York, Major,
that I wouldn't advise you to invade.

—RICK TO MAJOR STRASSER, *CASABLANCA*

In *Downtown: My Manhattan* (2004), Pete Hamill

I dream'd in a dream, I saw a city invincible to the
Attacks of the whole of the rest of the earth;

I dream'd that was the new City of Friends

—WHITMAN

In *Netherland* (2008), Joseph O'Neill

Fluellen: I think it is in Macedon where Alexander is born. I tell you, captain, if you look in the maps of the 'orld, I warrant you sall find, in the comparisons between Macedon and Monmouth, that the situations, look you, is both alike. There is a river in Macedon; and there is also moreover a river at Monmouth: it is called Wye at Monmouth; but it is out of my brains what is the name of the other river; but 'tis all one, 'tis alike as my fingers is to my fingers, and there is salmons in both.

—SHAKESPEARE, *KING HENRY THE FIFTH*

In *Black Lamb and Grey Falcon: A Journey Through Yugoslavia* (1941), Rebecca West

Rebecca West took three trips to Yugoslavia in the 1930s with the intention of writing a "snap" travel book that could be completed in a couple of months. Eventually reaching 1,200 pages, the book consumed five years of her life—and her soul. *Black Lamb and Grey Falcon* is an indelible, if digressive, portrait of Europe on the brink of war. As a travel guide to Yugoslavia, the peripatetic writer Geoff Dyer vouches for its continuing usefulness, calling West's classic "a kind of metaphysical *Lonely Planet* that never needs updating."

An oasis of horror in a desert of boredom.

—CHARLES BAUDELAIRE

In *2666* (2004), Roberto Bolaño

———————

It is because America has consented neither to sin nor to suffering that she has no soul.

—ANDRÉ GIDE

The destiny of France is to irritate the world.

—JEAN GIRAUDOUX

In *L'Affaire* (2003), Diane Johnson

And openly I pledged my heart to the grave
and suffering land, and often in the consecrated
night, I promised to love her faithfully until
death, unafraid, with her heavy burden of fa-
tality, and never to despise a single one of her
enigmas. Thus did I join myself to her with a
mortal cord.

—HÖLDERLIN: *THE DEATH OF EMPEDOCLES*

In *The Rebel* (1951), Albert Camus

The Rebel was the book that ended the close friendship
of Albert Camus and Jean-Paul Sartre, philosophers and
writers who had fought for the French Resistance in World
War II. The issue was communism. Sartre was for it, Camus
against. Their very public spat was carried out in the pages
of *Les Temps Modernes*, a journal edited by Sartre. It cul-
minated in an insult unlikely to be uttered beyond the *ter-
rasse* of Café de Flore: "I have at least this in common with
Hegel," Sartre wrote, "you have not read either one of us."
The two men never spoke again. Camus would die in a car
crash in 1960 after receiving the Nobel Prize for literature
in 1957.

She is not any common earth
    Water, or wood, or air
But Merlin's Isle of Gramarye
    Where you and I will fare.

In *The Once and Future King* (1958), T. H. White

White's unattributed epigraph comes from Rudyard Kipling's children's classic, *Puck of Pook's Hill.*

THE EMPIRE OF
THE MIND

The mind I love must have wild places, a tangled orchard where dark damsons drop in heavy grass, an overgrown little wood, the chance of a snake or two, a pool that nobody's fathomed the depth of, and paths threaded with flowers planted by the mind.

—KATHERINE MANSFIELD

In *Cocktail Hour Under the Tree of Forgetfulness* (2011), Alexandra Fuller

As long as hope maintains a thread of green.

—THE DIVINE COMEDY, PURGATORY, III

In *All the King's Men* (1946), Robert Penn Warren

So there is no fact, no event, in our private history, which shall not, sooner or later, lose its adhesive, inert form, and astonish us by soaring from our body into the empyrean? Cradle and infancy, school and playground, the fear of boys, and dogs, and ferules, the love of little maids and berries, and many another fact that once filled the whole sky, are gone already; friend and relative, profession and party, town and country, nation and world, must also soar and sing.

—RALPH WALDO EMERSON,
THE AMERICAN SCHOLAR

In *A Girl Named Zippy* (2001), Haven Kimmel

We are unhappy because we do not see how our unhappiness can end; whereas what we really fail to see is that unhappiness cannot last, since even a continuance of the same condition will bring about a change of mood. For the same reason happiness does not last.

—WILLIAM GERHARDIE, OF MORTAL LOVE

In *The City of Your Final Destination* (2002),
Peter Cameron

William Gerhardie was born in St. Petersburg, Russia, in 1895. His privileged, anglophile upbringing (and its abrupt termination with the Russian Revolution) was similar to that of his contemporary, Vladimir Nabokov, whom he would briefly meet years later in London. Sent to school in England, Gerhardie served with the British military during World War I and emerged as a novelist in the 1920s along with Evelyn Waugh, Aldous Huxley, and Anthony Powell. Edith Wharton wrote a preface to his first novel, and Graham Greene would later say, "To those of my generation, he was the most important new novelist to appear in our young life. We were proud of his early and immediate success, like men who have spotted the right horse." Gerhardie would publish no new work after 1939 and died in poverty and obscurity in 1977.

In the circle of light on the stage in the midst of darkness, you have the sensation of being entirely alone. . . . This is called solitude in public. . . . During a performance, before an audience of thousands, you can always enclose yourself in this circle, like a snail in its shell. . . . You can carry it wherever you go.

—CONSTANTIN STANISLAVSKI, *AN ACTOR PREPARES* (translated by Elizabeth Reynolds Hapgood)

In *Blonde* (2000), Joyce Carol Oates

PROSPERO: Every third thought shall be my grave.

—*THE TEMPEST, ACT V, SCENE I*

In *Sabbath's Theater* (1995), Philip Roth

For the thing which I greatly feared is come upon me, and that which I was afraid of is come unto me. I was not in safety, neither had I rest, neither was I quiet; yet trouble came.

—JOB

In *Darkness Visible* (1990), William Styron

At the age of sixty, Pulitzer Prize–winning novelist William Styron suffered a prolonged, suicidal depression that ultimately hospitalized him several times. Undaunted by the stigma of mental illness, Styron bravely published a candid memoir chronicling his struggles with the disease and subsequently became an advocate for fellow sufferers.

REBELS AND OUTSIDERS

If they give you ruled paper, write the other way.

—JUAN RAMÓN JIMÉNEZ

In *Fahrenheit 451* (1953), Ray Bradbury

Ray Bradbury wrote his dystopian classic in the basement library of UCLA, where typewriters could be rented by the half hour for a dime. Nine days and $9.80 later, he emerged with *Fahrenheit 451*. The epigraph is from the Spanish poet Juan Rámon Jiménez (1881–1958), who was forced into exile during the Spanish Civil War and awarded the Nobel Prize in 1956.

I will call them my people
Which were not my people;
And her beloved,
Which was not beloved.

—ROMANS 9:35

In *Beloved* (1987), Toni Morrison

Those who dance are considered insane by those
who can't hear the music.

—ANON.

In *Napalm & Silly Putty* (2001), George Carlin

For we are strangers before thee,
and sojourners, as were all our fathers.

—I CHRONICLES 29:15

In *Dreams from My Father: A Story of Race and Inheritance*
(1995), Barack Obama

For rebellion is as the sin of witchcraft.

—I SAMUEL 15:23

In *Outrageous Acts and Everyday Rebellions* (1983),
Gloria Steinem

They strike one, above all, as giving no account of themselves in any terms already consecrated by human use; to this inarticulate state they probably form, collectively, the most unprecedented of monuments; abysmal the mystery of what they think, what they feel, what they want, what they suppose themselves to be saying.

—HENRY JAMES

In *Another Country* (1962), James Baldwin

Mislike me not, for my complexion,
The shadowed livery of the burnished sun.

—*THE MERCHANT OF VENICE*, II.i.1–2

In *The Last of the Mohicans* (1826), James Fenimore Cooper

When a true genius appears in the world, you may know him by this sign, that the dunces are all in confederacy against him.

—JONATHAN SWIFT, "THOUGHTS ON VARIOUS SUBJECTS, MORAL AND DIVERTING"

In *A Confederacy of Dunces* (1980), John Kennedy Toole

After thirty-one-year-old John Kennedy Toole committed suicide in 1969, his mother would spend the next decade trying to get his manuscript, *A Confederacy of Dunces*, published. After countless rejections, she began pestering author Walker Percy, who eventually broke down and agreed to read it. Percy was so impressed that he convinced Louisiana State University Press to publish the novel, which went on to win the Pulitzer Prize in 1981.

You have navigated with raging soul far from the paternal home, passing beyond the seas' double rocks and now you inhabit a foreign land.

—*MEDEA*

In *The Passion* (1987), Jeanette Winterson

Even today is my complaint rebellious,
My stroke is heavier than my groaning.

—*JOB*

In *Native Son* (1940), Richard Wright

Satan, being thus confined to a vagabond, wandering, unsettled condition, is without any certain abode; for though he has, in consequence of his angelic nature, a kind of empire in the liquid waste or air, yet this is certainly part of his punishment that he is . . . without any fixed place, or space, allowed him to rest the sole of his foot upon.

—DANIEL DEFOE, *THE HISTORY OF THE DEVIL*

In *The Satanic Verses* (1988), Salman Rushdie

The locusts have no king, yet go they forth all of them by bands

—PROVERBS

In *The Locusts Have No King* (1948), Dawn Powell

"New York City is the only place where people with nothing behind them but their wits can be and do everything," wrote the Ohio-born novelist Dawn Powell in her diary. The city would be her great subject; one critic claimed Powell did for New York what Balzac had done for Paris. Gore Vidal would call Powell America's best comic novelist, but her life was beset by trouble. She drank; she maintained (with difficulty) an open marriage; her beloved son who would today be diagnosed with autism required constant care and was periodically institutionalized. Although critically acclaimed, her books brought her little money and she was perennially strapped for cash. Evicted from her Greenwich Village apartment, she lived precariously in a series of run-down hotels before her death in 1965. She is buried on Hart Island, New York City's potter's field.

THE
GENERATIONS

"You are young, sir," he said, "you are young; you are very very young, sir."

—*DAVID COPPERFIELD*

In *A Compass Error* (1968), Sybille Bedford

We have our secrets and our needs to confess. We may remember how, in childhood, adults were able at first to look right through us, and into us, and what an accomplishment it was when we, in fear and trembling, could tell our first lie, and make, for ourselves, the discovery that we are irredeemably alone in certain respects, and know that within the territory of ourselves, there can only be our own footprints.

—R. D. LAING, *THE DIVIDED SELF*

In *The Liars' Club* (1995), Mary Karr

But, child of dust, the fragrant flowers.
The bright blue sky and velvet sod
Were strange conductors to the bowers
Thy daring footsteps must have trod.

—EMILY BRONTË

In *The Go-Between* (1953), L. P. Hartley

Lawyers, I suppose, were children once.

—CHARLES LAMB

In *To Kill a Mockingbird* (1960), Harper Lee

"It was like being hit over the head and knocked out cold." That's how the famously private Lee described the phenomenal success of her first and only novel. In eschewing fame, Lee became famous as a literary recluse. Meanwhile, her book went on to become one of the best-selling novels of all time. Its epigraph comes from British essayist Charles Lamb (1775–1834), who undoubtedly had experience of lawyers, as his sister Mary stabbed and killed their mother in a fit of madness. Lamb stood loyally by Mary through the trial, and when she was found not guilty by reason of temporary insanity, the twenty-two-year-old Lamb took full legal responsibility for her for the rest of her life.

And this is how I see the East. . . . I see it always from a small boat—not a light, not a stir, not a sound. We conversed in low whispers, as if afraid to wake up the land. . . . It is all in that moment when I opened my young eyes on it. I came upon it from a tussle with the sea.

—JOSEPH CONRAD, *YOUTH*

In *The Cat's Table* (2011), Michael Ondaatje

Of course we need children! Adults need children in their lives to listen to and care for, to keep their imagination fresh and their hearts young and to make the future a reality for which they are willing to work.

—MARGARET MEAD

In *It Takes a Village* (1996), Hillary Rodham Clinton

At the age of twenty-two I believed myself to be unextinguishable.

—SIEGFRIED SASSOON, *MEMOIRS OF A FOX-HUNTING MAN*

In *The Good Times* (1989), Russell Baker

In middle age there is mystery, there is mystification. The most I can make out of this hour is a kind of loneliness. Even the beauty of the physical world seems to crumble, yes, even love.

—JOHN CHEEVER

In *The Good Life* (2006), Jay McInerney

I always had the idea that when I was old I'd get frightfully clever. I'd get awfully learned, I'd get jolly sage. People would come to me for advice. But nobody comes to me for anything, and I don't know a bloody thing.

—RALPH RICHARDSON

In *Another Life* (1999), Michael Korda

WE'RE ALL
MAD HERE

"If I wasn't real," Alice said—half-laughing through her tears, it all seemed so ridiculous—"I shouldn't be able to cry."

"I hope you don't suppose those are real tears?" Tweedledum interrupted in a tone of great contempt.

—*ALICE THROUGH THE LOOKING GLASS* (LEWIS CARROLL)

In *Vile Bodies* (1930), Evelyn Waugh

I want you to meet Miss Gorce, she's in the embalming game.

—JAMES THURBER (*MEN, WOMEN AND DOGS*)

In *The Dud Avocado* (1958), Elaine Dundy

Written in an attempt to save her marriage to theater critic Kenneth Tynan, Dundy's first novel became a further source of friction due to its success. Based on her experiences as an actress in Paris in the 1950s, Dundy claims that she wrote the novel by asking herself "What would I not do?" and then having her heroine Sally Jay Gorce do exactly that. Groucho Marx wrote her a fan letter, saying the novel "made me laugh, scream and guffaw (which incidentally is a great name for a law firm)."

This reminds me of the ludicrous account he gave Mr. Langton, of the despicable state of a young gentleman of good family. "Sir, when I heard of him last, he was running about town shooting cats." And then in a sort of kindly reverie, he bethought himself of his own favorite cat, and said, "But Hodge shan't be shot: no, no, Hodge shall not be shot."

—JAMES BOSWELL,
THE LIFE OF SAMUEL JOHNSON

In *Pale Fire* (1962), Vladimir Nabokov

Hodge survived the (possibly imagined) Great London Cat Massacre and is immortalized in a statue that stands outside Dr. Johnson's former home in Gough Square. As for Nabokov, his affection for cats was slightly less warm. He was once tormented by a noisy Siamese named Bandit who came with a house the writer rented in Ithaca, New York. In an effort to find peace, he would barricade himself in the study, but Bandit would only try to win Nabokov over by bringing in offerings of dead mice and playing hockey with the corpses against the study door.

That will ask some tears in the true perform-
ing of it: if I do it, let the audience look to their
eyes; I will move storms, I will condole in some
measure. . . . I could play Ercles rarely, or a part
to tear a cat in, to make all split . . . a lover is
more condoling.

—SHAKESPEARE,
A MIDSUMMER NIGHT'S DREAM

In *Busman's Honeymoon* (1937), Dorothy L. Sayers

"She reads at such a pace," she complained, "and when I asked her *where* she had learnt to read so quickly, she replied, 'On the screens at the Cinemas.'"

—*THE FLOWER BENEATH THE FOOT*

In *The Swimming-Pool Library* (1988), Alan Hollinghurst

Hollinghurst takes his epigraph from one of the novels of Ronald Firbank (1886–1926), a writer heavily influenced by Oscar Wilde. Because Firbank's novels were populated by gay and lesbian characters and dealt with frankly homosexual themes, no publisher in the pre– and post–World War I eras in which he was writing would touch them. He published his books at his own expense, and even though writers like E. M. Forster and Evelyn Waugh championed his work, critics ignored it. Thanks to later supporters like W. H. Auden, Susan Sontag (who cited Firbank's novels as belonging to the "canon of camp" in her 1964 essay, "Notes on Camp"), and Hollinghurst, Firbank maintains a cult following.

The houses are all gone under the sea.

—T. S. ELIOT

In *Monkeys* (1986), Susan Minot

LADY BRACKNELL: . . . Are your parents living?
JACK: I have lost both my parents.
LADY BRACKNELL: Both? . . . To lose one
   parent, Mr. Worthing, may be regarded
   as a misfortune; to lose both looks like
   carelessness.

—OSCAR WILDE, *THE IMPORTANCE
OF BEING EARNEST*

In *Losing Mum and Pup* (2009), Christopher Buckley

There is pleasure sure
In being mad, which none but mad men know.
—DRYDEN, *THE SPANISH FRIAR*, II, i

In *My Family and Other Animals* (1956), Gerald Durrell

While his older brother Lawrence Durrell, author of *The Alexandria Quartet*, was famous for collecting women, Gerald became famous for collecting animals. A pioneering naturalist and conservationist, Gerald Durrell began traveling to remote regions of the world to collect animals for British zoos beginning in 1946. In the 1950s, on the Channel Island of Jersey, he founded the first zoo to house only endangered species.

An Excellent
Thing in a Woman

Since I can do no good because a woman,
Reach constantly at something that is near it.

—THE MAID'S TRAGEDY:
BEAUMONT AND FLETCHER

In *Middlemarch* (1871–1872), George Eliot

George Eliot (pseudonym of Marian Evans) chose to evoke the struggles of her heroine Dorothea Brooke with these lines from a seventeenth-century play by Francis Beaumont and John Fletcher, members of the King's Men—the company of actors to which Shakespeare belonged for most of his career.

She's not pretty, she's not wearing rouge.

—SAINTE-BEUVE

In *The Red and the Black* (1830), Stendhal

Today the combat takes a different shape; instead of wishing to put man in a prison, woman endeavors to escape from one; she no longer seeks to drag him into the realms of immanence but to emerge, herself, into the light of transcendence. Now the attitude of males creates a new conflict: it is with a bad grace that the man lets her go.

—SIMONE DE BEAUVOIR, *THE SECOND SEX*

In *The Stepford Wives* (1972), Ira Levin

She was her parents' only joy:
They had but one—one darling child.

—*ROMEO AND JULIET*

In *Charlotte Temple* (1790), Susanna Rowson

This story of a fifteen-year-old British girl seduced by a soldier, taken to America, and abandoned there became the first American best seller. Often dismissed by critics as mere sentimental fiction, the novel exerted a powerful hold on the American imagination for generations. Well into the twentieth century, fans would flock to Trinity Churchyard in New York City, leaving flowers and letters on a grave marked by a tombstone inscribed "Charlotte Temple." No records survive to clear up the mystery of who is buried there, but Rowson deserves credit for creating a character so believable that many readers were convinced she actually existed.

bach·e·lor (bach'ə ler, bach'lər) n. 3. a fur seal, esp. a young male, kept from the breeding grounds by the older males.

bach'elor girl, an unmarried woman, esp. a young one, who supports herself and often lives alone. [1890–95]

—THE RANDOM HOUSE DICTIONARY
OF THE ENGLISH LANGUAGE,
SECOND EDITION, UNABRIDGED

In *Bachelor Girls* (1990), Wendy Wasserstein

We had certainly luck in finding good cooks, though they had their weaknesses in other ways. Gertrude Stein liked to remind me that if they did not have such faults, they would not be working for us.

—ALICE B. TOKLAS

In *The Book of Salt* (2003), Monique Truong

Toklas herself was no slouch in the kitchen. American chef and culinary expert James Beard praised her as "one of the really great cooks of all time . . . her chicken dishes were especially magnificent."

I have the heart of a man, not of a woman, and
I am not afraid of anything . . .

—ELIZABETH I, QUEEN OF ENGLAND

In *A Woman of Substance* (1979), Barbara Taylor Bradford

Rise up, ye women that are at ease! Hear my
voice, ye careless daughters! Give ear unto my
speech.

—ISAIAH XXXII.9

In *Incidents in the Life of a Slave Girl, Written by Herself*
(1861), Harriet Jacobs

High rouged, unfortunate female of whom it is
not proper to speak without necessity.

—THOMAS CARLYLE

In *Madame de Pompadour* (1954), Nancy Mitford

Mitford had a sparkling reputation and large following as a
comic novelist, but when it came to writing her first work
of historical biography, she worried about finding the right
"voice"—and her lack of credentials. Her friend Evelyn
Waugh advised her: "Write for the sort of reader who knows
Louis XV furniture when she sees it, but thinks Louis XV
was the son of Louis XIV and had his head cut off."

Alas! the love of women! it is known
      To be a lovely and a fearful thing;
For all of theirs upon that die is thrown,
      And if 'tis lost, life hath no more to bring
To them but mockeries of the past alone,
      And their revenge is as the tiger's spring,
Deadly, and quick, and crushing; yet, as real
Torture is theirs—what they inflict they feel.

They are right; for man, to man so oft unjust,
      Is always so to women; one sole bond
Awaits them—treachery is all their trust;
      Taught to conceal, their bursting hearts
      despond
Over their idol, till some wealthier lust
      Buys them in marriage—and what rests
      beyond?

A thankless husband—next a faithless lover—
Then dressing, nursing, praying—and all's
	over.

Some take a lover, some take drams or prayers,
		Some mind their household, others
			dissipation,
Some run away, and but exchange their cares,
		Losing the advantage of a virtuous
			station;
Few changes e'er can better their affairs,
		Theirs being an unnatural situation,
From the dull palace to the dirty hovel:
Some play the devil, and then write a novel.
		—LORD BYRON (FROM DON JUAN)

In *Fear of Flying* (1973), Erica Jong

... as for this little lady, the best thing I can wish her is a *little misfortune*.

—WILLIAM MAKEPEACE THACKERAY

In *A Widow for One Year* (1998), John Irving

[The history of most women is] hidden either by silence, or by flourishes and ornaments that amount to silence.

—VIRGINIA WOOLF

In *Ornament and Silence* (1996), Kennedy Fraser

KNOW THYSELF

To be happy you must have taken the measure
of your powers, tasted the fruits of your passion,
and learned your place in the world.

—SANTAYANA

In *The Gastronomical Me* (1943), M. F. K. Fisher

"M. F. K. Fisher writes about food as others do about love,
but only better." That was the pronouncement of preeminent literary critic Clifton Fadiman. Fisher pioneered the
culinary memoir in pre–Julia Child America. No mean
feat. She resisted pressure to write novels and other more
conventional and commercial kinds of books, arguing that
"There is a communion of more than our bodies when
bread is broken and wine is drunk." W. H. Auden considered her America's best prose writer.

Therefore I am unhappy and it is neither my fault nor that of life.

—JULES LAFORGUE

In *Three Lives* (1909), Gertrude Stein

Others merely live, I vegetate.

—CYRIL CONNOLLY, *THE UNQUIET GRAVE*

In *Alice in Bed* (1983), Cathleen Schine

Poets claim that we recapture for a moment the self that we were long ago when we enter the same house or garden in which we used to live in our youth. But these are the most hazardous pilgrimages, which end as often as not in disappointment as in success. It is in ourselves that we should rather seek to find those fixed places, contemporaneous with different years.

The unknown element in the lives of other people is like that of nature, which each fresh scientific discovery merely reduces but does not abolish.

—MARCEL PROUST, *IN SEARCH OF LOST TIME*

In *A Visit from the Goon Squad* (2010), Jennifer Egan

Child, knowledge is a treasury and your heart
its strongbox.

—HUGO OF ST. VICTOR, from *THE THREE
BEST MEMORY AIDS FOR LEARNING HISTORY*

In *The Memory Palace* (2011), Mira Bartók

Hugo (also known as "Hugh") of St. Victor was a twelfth-
century mystic and theologian, a contemporary of Peter
Abelard. Hugo arrived at the Abbey of Saint Victor in Paris
in 1115. Although he wrote on a wide range of topics, including history, philosophy, grammar, and geometry, it was
as a teacher that Hugo became famous. Under his direction,
the school of the Victorine Abbey was renowned through-
out Europe, and Hugo is credited with designing a course
of study that would be adopted throughout the medieval
university system.

Does the Siberian ask heaven for olive trees, or the Provençal for cranberries?

—JOSEPH DE MAISTRE,
LES SOIRÉES DE ST. PETERSBOURG

In *Dreams of My Russian Summer* (1995), Andreï Makine

When he hath tried me, I shall come forth as gold.

—JOB

In *Breakfast of Champions* (1973), Kurt Vonnegut

Montaigne says that men go open to future things: I have the idiosyncrasy of being open to things past.

In *The Garden Party* (1922), Katherine Mansfield

That Mansfield looked to the past rather than the future is perhaps not surprising, given that she would die young, at age thirty-four, the year after *The Garden Party*'s publication. Tuberculosis was the cause, and scholars speculate that she may have contracted it from her friend, D. H. Lawrence. Another friend, Virginia Woolf, would write in her diary after Mansfield's death, "I was jealous of her writing—the only writing I have ever been jealous of."

Beauteous art, brought with us from heaven,
will conquer nature; so divine a power
belongs to him who strives with every nerve.

If I was made for art, from childhood given
a prey for burning beauty to devour,
I blame the mistress I was born to serve.

—MICHELANGELO BUONARROTI

In *The Agony and the Ecstasy* (1961), Irving Stone

Surely, of all things in the world the rarest is a civilized man at peace with himself.

—GONTRAN DE PONCINS, *KABLOONA*

In *A Big Storm Knocked It Over* (1993), Laurie Colwin

An aristocratic Frenchman (and descendent of Michel de Montaigne), Gontran de Poncins (1900–1962) was an adventurer who recounted his experiences living among the Inuit in the Canadian Arctic in *Kabloona*, published in 1941. "Kabloona" is a transcription of a semi-derogatory Inuit word used to describe white Europeans. Living an almost Stone Age existence in an inhospitable landscape for fifteen months, de Poncins struggled and nearly died. The end result was a spiritual awakening that left him questioning the values of the "civilized" world he left behind.

Is it not the chief disgrace in the world, not to be a unit;—not to be reckoned one character;—not to yield that peculiar fruit which each man was created to bear, but to be reckoned in the gross, in the hundred, or the thousand, of the party, the section, to which we belong . . .

—RALPH WALDO EMERSON

In *Then We Came to the End* (2007), Joshua Ferris

Yes, there were times when I forgot not only who I was, but that I was, forgot to be.

—SAMUEL BECKETT, *MOLLOY*

In *The Feast of Love* (2000), Charles Baxter

Nobody knew my rose of the world but me. . . .
I had too much glory. They don't want glory like
that in nobody's heart.

—THE ROSE TATTOO

In *Sula* (1973), Toni Morrison

PARADOX

To find the soul it is necessary to lose it.

—A. R. LURIA

In *The Echo Maker* (2006), Richard Powers

Aleksandr Romanovich Luria (1902–1977) pioneered the field of neuropsychology in the 1930s and '40s. Although Stalinist purges and anti-Semitic repression would interrupt his research at various points, Luria's work on brain trauma prompted Oliver Sacks to write: "Luria's case histories can only be compared to Freud's . . . [B]oth explore, fundamentally, the nature of man; both are new ways of thinking about human nature."

The challenge of modernity is to live without illusions and without becoming disillusioned.

—ANTONIO GRAMSCI

In *The Believers* (2009), Zoë Heller

This too is probable, according to that saying of Agathon: It is part of probability that many improbable things will happen.

—ARISTOTLE: *POETICS*

In *Daniel Deronda* (1876), George Eliot

The sinner is at the very heart of Christianity . . .
No one is as competent as the sinner in Christian affairs. No one, except the saint.

—PÉGUY

In *The Heart of the Matter* (1948), Graham Greene

The Catholic convert Greene turns to another Catholic convert, Charles Péguy (1873–1914), for his epigraph. Péguy was a noted French poet (T. S. Eliot and André Gide were fans) who started a journal to champion socialist causes, although, as one commentator noted, his socialism was more akin to that of Saint Francis than that of Karl Marx. An atheist, Péguy stunned his friends by announcing his return to the Catholic faith—although he would remain hostile to the Church as an institution. He is credited with reviving the tradition of making the pilgrimage to Chartres cathedral on foot. When World War I was declared, Péguy immediately enlisted and was killed on the first day of the Battle of the Marne.

Nothing lasts, and yet nothing passes, either.
And nothing passes just because nothing lasts.
—PHILIP ROTH, *THE HUMAN STAIN*

In *Truth & Beauty* (2004), Ann Patchett

His honour rooted in dishonour stood,
And faith unfaithful kept him falsely true.
—ALFRED, LORD TENNYSON

In *I'll Be Seeing You* (1993), Mary Higgins Clark

… and so who are
You after all?
—I am part of the power Which forever wills
  evil
And forever works good.

—GOETHE'S FAUST

In *The Master and Margarita* (1967), Mikhail Bulgakov

Mikhail Bulgakov (1891–1940) was a Russian novelist and playwright who found himself engaged in a tortuous cat-and-mouse game with the dictator Joseph Stalin. Stalin loved Bulgakov's work (he saw one play fifteen times) but banned most of it. By 1929, Bulgakov was desperate, broke, and denied emigration. Stalin's favor protected him from arrest and execution, but the threat of both remained ever present. He began writing *The Master and Margarita*, a satire of Soviet life in which the devil and his retinue descend on Moscow. Paranoid, fearing exposure, he would burn the manuscript; and then spend much of the 1930s rewriting it from memory before his early death in 1940. It would be more than twenty-five years before the *The Master and Margarita* appeared in print. After reading the newly published novel, Mick Jagger would write the Rolling Stones classic "Sympathy for the Devil."

Verily, verily, I say unto you, Except a corn of wheat fall into the ground and die, it abideth alone: but if it die, it bringeth forth much fruit.

—JOHN 12:24

In *The Brothers Karamazov* (1880), Fyodor Dostoevsky

Art is a lie which makes us realize the truth.

—PICASSO

In *My Name Is Asher Lev* (1972), Chaim Potok

The Messiah will only come when he is no longer needed

—FRANZ KAFKA

In *Skinny Legs and All* (1990), Tom Robbins

———————

It is only shallow people who do not judge by appearances. The mystery of the world is the visible, not the invisible.

—OSCAR WILDE, IN A LETTER

In *Against Interpretation and Other Essays* (1966), Susan Sontag

Food to the indolent is poison, not sustenance.
—*LIFE AND TIMES OF FREDERICK DOUGLASS*

In *Rabbit at Rest* (1990), John Updike

With love and care the spiderweb weaves its spider.

—AFRICAN PROVERB

In *The Fifth Woman* (1996), Henning Mankell

WIT AND WISDOM

The secret of being a bore is to say everything.

—VOLTAIRE

In *A Suitable Boy* (1993), Vikram Seth

The first duty in life is to assume a pose. What the second is, no one has yet discovered.

—OSCAR WILDE

In *This Boy's Life* (1989), Tobias Wolff

Behind every great fortune there is a crime.

—BALZAC

In *The Godfather* (1969), Mario Puzo

"I was 45-years-old, I owed $20,000 to relatives, finance companies, banks and assorted bookmakers and loan sharks. It was really time to grow up and sell out." Mario Puzo was not the first author to write something solely for money, but few have succeeded in that aim so spectacularly. *The Godfather* sold twenty-one million copies even *before* the blockbuster film version was released. Son of illiterate Italian immigrants, Puzo grew up in New York's Hell's Kitchen. His father abandoned the family, leaving his mother to raise seven children alone. She was an exceptionally dignified and determined person and Puzo has said he based the character of Don Corleone on her. "Whenever the Godfather opened his mouth, in my own mind I heard the voice of my mother."

Why does everybody pick on the economists? They've correctly predicted thirteen of the past five recessions!

—FAMILIAR CAMPUS JOKE

In *New England White* (2007), Stephen L. Carter

If you can see, look. If you can look, observe.

—FROM THE *BOOK OF EXHORTATIONS*

In *Blindness* (1995), José Saramago

Look for the ridiculous in everything and you will find it.

—JULES RENARD, 1890

In *Running with Scissors* (2002), Augusten Burroughs

"Directly, or indirectly, Renard is at the origin of contemporary literature," proclaimed Jean-Paul Sartre. Certainly, there are affinities between Burroughs's memoir of his chaotic upbringing and Renard's 1894 semiautobiographical novel, *Poile de Carotte* (Carrot Top), about a clever child making his way in the world despite his cruel and indifferent family. Although Renard (1864–1910) wrote numerous poems, novels, and plays, he is most famous for his diaries, published fifteen years after his death. These journals are filled with epigrams and other clever sayings, such as "I am never bored anywhere; being bored is an insult to oneself" and "The only man who is really free is the one who can turn down an invitation to dinner without giving an excuse."

The heart is half a prophet.

—YIDDISH PROVERB

In *Goodbye, Columbus* (1959), Philip Roth

Weeping may endure for a night, but joy cometh in the morning.

—PSALMS 30:5

In *Joy in the Morning* (1963), Betty Smith

> The grandeur of the soul does not consist in
> flying high, but in walking orderly; its grandeur
> does not exercise in grandeur, but in mediocrity.
>
> —MONTAIGNE

In *Memoirs of a Public Baby* (1958), Philip O'Connor

There are few figures as strange as Philip O'Connor (1916–
1998) in the annals of English literature. A surrealist poet,
his behavior could also be surreal, as when he jumped out
from behind a door and yelled "Boo!" at T. S. Eliot. He was
described in an obituary "as thin as a skeleton, his face already eroded, his smile never calm, he lived off donuts and
Woodbines, ogled at women and spoke in cryptograms,
spoonerisms and jingles, delivering sentences backwards
and falling about in drunken exhilaration." All this is perhaps understandable upon reading his memoir. His mother
abandoned him in the care of a woman who ran a pastry
shop, reclaiming him a few years later, only to abandon him
again, this time with a one-legged civil servant. *Memoirs of
a Public Baby* drew praise from William S. Burroughs, Paul
Bowles, and Dorothy Parker. O'Connor became a radio
personality in the 1960s. He interviewed Quentin Crisp,
who credited O'Connor with "inventing" him.

MORALITY

Through tattered clothes small vices do
    appear;
Robes and furred gowns hide all.
Plate sin with gold,
And the strong lance of justice hurtless breaks;
Arm it in rags, a pygmy's straw does pierce it.

—*KING LEAR*

In *Small Vices* (1997), Robert B. Parker

But I say unto you, That whosoever looketh on a woman to lust after her hath committed adultery with her already in his heart.

—MATTHEW V, 28

In *The Kreutzer Sonata* (1889), Leo Tolstoy

At the time Tolstoy was writing this tale in which a man discovers his wife is unfaithful and murders her, he came to believe that "Christian marriage" was a contradiction in terms and that chastity was the ultimate ideal of humanity. Needless to say, his wife was not amused. The marriage that produced *War and Peace*, *Anna Karenina*, and *The Kreutzer Sonata* was perhaps the unhappiest in literary history. While the novella was intended to argue for celibacy, all the censors saw was a frank description of female sexuality, and the book was banned in Russia and much of the United States. Reviewing *The Kreutzer Sonata* in England, G. K. Chesterton, recognized its merits but cautioned its author: "You are at least next door to hating humanity."

Virtues are forced upon us by our impudent crimes.

—T. S. ELIOT

In *The Tunnel of Love* (1954), Peter De Vries

"Every good novel must have a beginning, a muddle, and an end," quipped Peter De Vries, a mid-twentieth-century comic novelist once described as "P.G. Wodehouse in Connecticut." De Vries worked for *The New Yorker* for over thirty years writing humor pieces and serving as "cartoon doctor," improving captions and coming up with funny lines for artists to illustrate. In describing his particular brand of humor, De Vries said: "The satirist shoots to kill while the humorist brings his prey back alive and eventually releases him again for another chance."

We should esteem the man who is liberal, not the man who decides to be so.

—MACHIAVELLI

In *Cultural Amnesia* (2007), Clive James

What song the Syrenes sang, or what name Achilles assumed when he hid himself among women, although puzzling questions, are not beyond *all* conjecture.

—SIR THOMAS BROWNE, *URN-BURIAL*

In "The Murders in the Rue Morgue" (1841), Edgar Allan Poe

And what is good, Phaedrus,
And what is not good—
Need we ask anyone to tell us these things?

In *Zen and the Art of Motorcycle Maintenance* (1974),
Robert M. Pirsig

Pirsig's epigraph is an allusion to one of Plato's dialogues,
the *Phaedrus*.

Conventionality is not morality. Self-righteousness is not religion. To attack the first is not to assail the last.

—CHARLOTTE BRONTË

In *The Cider House Rules* (1985), John Irving

People pay for what they do, and still more, for what they have allowed themselves to become. And they pay for it simply: by the lives they lead.

—JAMES BALDWIN

In *Bastard Out of Carolina* (1992), Dorothy Allison

The quality of mercy . . .

　　　　　　　　is twice bless'd;
It blesseth him that gives, and him that takes;
'Tis mightiest in the mightiest: it becomes
The thronèd monarch better than his crown.

　　　　　　　　　　—*MERCHANT OF VENICE*

In *The Prince and the Pauper* (1882), Mark Twain

Twain did not believe that Shakespeare wrote the famous plays; thus, it's not surprising that he omits the Bard of Avon's name when identifying the epigraph. A proponent of the theory that Francis Bacon (Elizabethan-era philosopher, scientist, author, lawyer, and Lord Chancellor of England) was the true author of the plays, Twain published a pamphlet entitled *Is Shakespeare Dead?* in 1909. In it, he scoffs at the idea that Will Shakespeare, merely by serving a brief stint as clerk at Stratford Court, could have amassed the vast knowledge of the law that the plays demonstrate. Twain claims that such a feat would be as preposterous as his having complete and perfect knowledge of the Bering Strait whaling industry simply by being raised on the banks of the Mississippi River.

When Perdikkas asked him at what times he wished to have divine honors paid him, he answered that he wished it done when they themselves were happy. These were the last words of the king.

—QUINTUS CURTIUS

In *Fire from Heaven* (1969), Mary Renault

Brothers, men who live after us,
Let not your hearts be hardened against us,
Because, if you have pity for us poor men,
God will have more mercy toward you.

—FRANÇOIS VILLON,
"BALLAD OF THE HANGED MAN"

In *In Cold Blood* (1966), Truman Capote

In April 1965, Dick Hickock and Perry Smith were hanged for the murders of four members of the Clutter family of Holcomb, Kansas. Truman Capote immersed himself in the case to produce the classic, *In Cold Blood*, becoming close to Hickock and Smith in the process. Fifteenth-century French poet François Villon composed his *Ballade des Pendus* while in prison awaiting his own execution by hanging. Villon had killed a priest in a street brawl while still a student, but escaped the death penalty that time because the priest publicly forgave him before dying. A thief and a brawler, Villon was banished and imprisoned multiple times before a church-robbing incident led to a death sentence. At the last minute, his sentence was commuted to ten years banishment. King Louis XI reportedly said, "I cannot afford to hang François Villon. There are a hundred thousand rogues in France as great as he, but not another such poet."

A MATTER OF
PERCEPTION

The madman runs to the East
And his keeper runs to the East;
Both are running to the East.
Their purposes differ.

—ZEN PROVERB

In *Running to the Mountain* (1999), Jon Katz

The General, speaking one felt with authority, always insisted that, if you bring off adequate preservation of your personal myth, nothing much else in life matters. It is not what happens to people that is significant, but what they think happens to them.

—ANTHONY POWELL,
BOOKS DO FURNISH A ROOM

In *The Emperor's Children* (2006), Claire Messud

Widely regarded as "the English Proust," Anthony Powell is the author of a twelve-volume masterpiece, *A Dance to the Music of Time* (of which *Books Do Furnish a Room* is the tenth novel in the series), inspired by seventeenth-century French artist Nicolas Poussin's great allegorical painting of the same name. Written between 1950 and 1975, the novels present an intricately detailed portrait of upper-middle-class British life in the twentieth century.

Not all who wander are lost.

—J. R. R. TOLKIEN

In *The Sisterhood of the Traveling Pants* (2001),
Ann Brashares

Life goes into new forms.

—NEAL CASSADY

In *Resuscitation of a Hanged Man* (1991), Denis Johnson

The motions of Grace, the hardness of the heart; external circumstances.

—PASCAL, PENSÉE 507

In *Rabbit, Run* (1960), John Updike

Today, Blaise Pascal (1623–1662) is most famous for his philosophical *Pensées*, but it was as a mathematician that he made his mark on the seventeenth century. A child prodigy, he invented an early form of the calculator, the Pascaline, while still a teenager. He worked on probability theory with Pierre de Fermat and was involved in the invention of the barometer with Evangelista Torricelli. But in 1650 he suddenly abandoned scientific pursuits and dedicated himself to contemplating "the greatness and misery of man." None of Pascal's philosophical works were published in his lifetime. *Pensées* appeared in 1669, seven years after his death.

If the doors of perception were cleansed everything would appear to man as it is, infinite.

—WILLIAM BLAKE

In *The Doors of Perception* (1954), Aldous Huxley

There's only a thin red line between the sane and
the mad.

—OLD MIDDLEWESTERN SAYING

In *The Thin Red Line* (1962), James Jones

Human existence being an hallucination containing in itself the secondary hallucinations of day and night (the latter an insanitary condition of the atmosphere due to accretions of black air), it ill becomes any man of sense to be concerned at the illusory approach of the supreme hallucination known as death.

—DE SELBY

In *The Third Policeman* (1967), Flann O'Brien

"De Selby" is the fictional creation of Flann O'Brien, who is the fictional creation of Irish civil servant Brian O'Nolan (1911–1966). De Selby, the philosopher and scientist whom O'Brien puts at the heart of *The Third Policeman*, believes that instead of being round, the earth is actually shaped like a sausage, among other nonsensical theories. Completed in 1940, *The Third Policeman* was turned down by O'Brien's publisher. After a halfhearted attempt to secure another, he gave up and put the novel on a shelf, where it sat for twenty-six years. After O'Brien's death, the manuscript was found and published to great acclaim.

The concrete world has slipped through the meshes of the scientific net.

—ALFRED NORTH WHITEHEAD,
MODES OF THOUGHT

In *Communion: A True Story* (1987), Whitley Strieber

What they call dying is merely the last pain.

—AMBROSE BIERCE

In *The Old Gringo* (1985), Carlos Fuentes

Who sees variety and not the Unity wanders on
from death to death

—BRIHAD-ARANYAKA UPANISHAD

In *Middle Passage* (1990), Charles Johnson

A Buddhist with a doctorate in philosophy, Charles Johnson offers a fresh perspective on the subject of slavery in
his prize-winning novel, *Middle Passage*. "Racism is based
on our belief in a division between Self and Other," Johnson said in an interview, echoing the message of his novel's
epigraph. Comprising more than two hundred texts, the
Upanishads form the core of Indian philosophy, elucidat-
ing concepts of karma, soul, nirvana, and reincarnation.
Written in Sanskrit by multiple anonymous authors, the
Upanishads were composed primarily between 800 and
400 B.C., although some texts date from much later. The
Brihad-aranyaka Upanishad quoted in Johnson's epigraph
is one of the oldest and longest texts. Tolstoy, Schopen-
hauer, Emerson, Thoreau, and Whitman are among the
Western authors deeply influenced by the Upanishads.

All one could do was to glimpse, amid the haze and chimeras, something real ahead, just as persons endowed with an unusual persistence of diurnal cerebration are able to perceive in their deepest sleep, somewhere beyond the throes of an entangled and inept nightmare, the ordered reality of the waking hour.

—VLADIMIR NABOKOV, *SPEAK, MEMORY*

In *Two Girls, Fat and Thin* (1991), Mary Gaitskill

Books and Storytelling

A novel—a small tale, generally of love
— DR. JOHNSON'S *DICTIONARY*

In *A Month in the Country* (1980), J. L. Carr

Go then, my little Book, and show to all
That entertain, and bid thee welcome shall
What Thou dost keep close shut up in thy breast;
And wish what thou dost show them may be blest
To them for good, may make them choose to be
Pilgrims better, by far, than thee or me.
Tell them of Mercy; she is one
Who early hath her pilgrimage begun.
Yea, yet young damsels learn of her to prize
The world which is to come, and so be wise;
For little tripping maids may follow God
Along the ways which saintly feet have trod.

—ADAPTED FROM JOHN BUNYAN

In *Little Women* (1868–1869), Louisa May Alcott

Alcott opens her classic novel with the four March sisters remembering how as small children they used to play "Pilgrim's Progress," from John Bunyan's 1678 Christian allegory. Bunyan, a Puritan and preacher, wrote his novel in verse while serving a twelve-year prison sentence for "preaching without a license." Alcott no doubt identified with his unsanctioned spirituality. Born to a Unitarian mother and Quaker father, part of the Transcendentalist circle in Concord, Massachusetts, Alcott never joined a church, but had a profound sense of morality and duty that led her to volunteer as a nurse during the Civil War and to assume financial responsibility for her family, lifting them out of poverty through her writing.

Let other pens dwell on guilt and misery.

—*MANSFIELD PARK*

In *Cold Comfort Farm* (1932), Stella Gibbons

———————

I do not propose to write an ode to dejection, but to brag as lustily as chanticleer in the morning, standing on his roost, if only to wake my neighbors up.

In *Walden* (1854), Henry David Thoreau

Thoreau's epigraph is taken from Chapter Two of *Walden*, "Where I Lived, and What I Lived For."

I shall be telling this with a sigh . . .

—ROBERT FROST, "THE ROAD NOT TAKEN"

In *Anagrams* (1986), Lorrie Moore

These novels will give way, by and by, to diaries or autobiographies—captivating books, if only a man knew how to choose among what he calls his experiences that which is really his experience, and how to record truth truly.

—RALPH WALDO EMERSON

In *Tropic of Cancer* (1934), Henry Miller

In these random impressions, and with no desire to be other than random, I indifferently narrate my factless autobiography, my lifeless history. These are my Confessions, and if in them I say nothing, it's because I have nothing to say.

—TEXT 12

In *The Book of Disquiet* (1982), Fernando Pessoa

The Portuguese author Pessoa's epigraph is taken from his own modernist masterpiece, which famously languished in a trunk for decades before being published forty-seven years after his death. Fernando Pessoa (1888–1935) wrote under dozens of pseudonyms and created elaborate identities for his fictional alter egos. For *The Book of Disquiet*, he chose "Bernardo Soares, assistant bookkeeper in the city of Lisbon."

The reader should realize himself that it could not have happened otherwise, and that to give him any other name was quite out of the question.

—NIKOLAI GOGOL, "THE OVERCOAT"

In *The Namesake* (2003), Jhumpa Lahiri

Come then, and let us pass a leisure hour in storytelling, and our story shall be the education of our heroes.

—PLATO, *REPUBLIC*, BOOK II

In *The Secret History* (1992), Donna Tartt

I like you and your book, ingenious Hone!
In whose capacious all-embracing leaves
The very marrow of tradition's shown.

—CHARLES LAMB, "TO THE EDITOR
OF THE EVERY-DAY BOOK"

In *The Marrow of Tradition* (1901), Charles W. Chesnutt

An early voice in African American fiction, Charles Chesnutt (1858–1932) was also an activist who worked alongside W. E. B. Du Bois and Booker T. Washington in various campaigns to promote racial equality.

To begin with death. To work my way back into life, and then, finally, to return to death. Or else: the vanity of trying to say anything about anyone.

—PAUL AUSTER, *THE INVENTION OF SOLITUDE*

In *Brother, I'm Dying* (2007), Edwidge Danticat

———————

"Of course," concluded Robert Kilburn Root, sitting crosslegged and contemplating his *shashlik*—"of course if this book is well larded with anecdotes, it will of necessity be short."

In *Serve It Forth* (1937), M. F. K. Fisher

The inimitable stories of Tong-king never have any real ending, and this one, being in his most elevated style, has even less end than most of them. But the whole narrative is permeated with the odour of joss-sticks and honourable high-mindedness, and the two characters are both of noble birth.

—*THE WALLET OF KAI-LUNG*

In *Clouds of Witness* (1926), Dorothy L. Sayers

One of the stars of the "Golden Age" of detective fiction, Dorothy Sayers (1893–1957) was among the first women to graduate from Oxford University. In the 1920s she worked for a London advertising agency, where she was responsible for the Colman's mustard and Guinness stout campaigns. She introduced her famous sleuth, Lord Peter Wimsey, in the 1923 novel *Whose Body?* An aristocrat and World War I veteran, Wimsey was intended to be a combination of Fred Astaire and P. J. Wodehouse's Bertie Wooster, according to Sayers. Her epigraph here comes from Ernest Bramah, the reclusive author of popular faux-Chinese adventure stories, as well as mystery and science fiction novels.

Novels arise out of the shortcomings of history.
—F. VON HARDENBERG, LATER NOVALIS,
FRAGMENTE UND STUDIEN, 1799–1800

In *The Blue Flower* (1995), Penelope Fitzgerald

Troubles overcome are good to tell.
—YIDDISH PROVERB

In *The Periodic Table* (1975), Primo Levi

This book is essentially different from any other that has been published concerning the "late war" or any of its incidents. Those who have had any such experience as the author will see its truthfulness at once, and to all other readers it is commended as a statement of actual things by one who experienced them to the fullest.

—*JOHN RANSOM'S ANDERSONVILLE DIARY*

In *The Things They Carried* (1990), Tim O'Brien

Persons attempting to find a motive in this narrative will be prosecuted; persons attempting to find a moral in it will be banished; persons attempting to find a plot in it will be shot.

—BY ORDER OF THE AUTHOR PER G.G.,
CHIEF OF ORDNANCE

In *Adventures of Huckleberry Finn* (1885), Mark Twain

Although not technically an epigraph, this humorous warning is the first thing readers encounter when opening *Huckleberry Finn*, the book from which all modern American literature descends, according to Ernest Hemingway. Twain would have needed a lot of firepower to follow through on his threats, as the novel's motives and morals have been questioned from the moment of publication. It was immediately banned from the Concord Public Library in Massachusetts, which deemed it "the veriest trash, suitable only for slums." Huck's grammar and hygiene were cited as causes for the book being banned from the Brooklyn Public Library in 1905. In the 1950s, the book began being contested for racial slurs. It was even removed from the Mark Twain Intermediate School in Fairfax, Virginia. A leading African American civil rights organization, the NAACP, takes the position that "you don't ban Mark Twain—you explain Mark Twain. To study an idea is not necessarily to endorse an idea . . . *Huckleberry Finn* portrays a time in history—the nineteenth century—and one of its evils, slavery."

BITTER TRUTH

O scathful harm, condition of poverte!

—CHAUCER

In *Down and Out in Paris and London* (1933),
George Orwell

> To sorrow
> I bade a good morrow,
> And thought to leave her far away behind;
> But cheerly, cheerly,
> She loves me dearly;
> She is so constant to me, and so kind.
> I would deceive her,
> And so leave her,
> But ah! She is so constant and so kind.

In *The Return of the Native* (1878), Thomas Hardy

How to account for the unrelenting pessimism in Thomas Hardy's fiction? Even his most sympathetic biographer likened reading *Jude the Obscure* to "being hit in the face over and over again." A highly sensitive man, Hardy no doubt suffered as his books were attacked in the press for being immoral and too darkly fatalistic. Booksellers deemed his novels so risqué that they were frequently sold in brown paper bags. Still, none of this caused him to change his tune. Vexed editors tried to get him to tone down the sex and the gloom. Leslie Stephen, editor of *The Cornhill Magazine* and the father of Virginia Woolf, chided, "You may not have to consider the vicar's daughters, but I do." Hardy doesn't identify it, but the epigraph here comes from Keats's "Ode to Sorrow in *Endymion*." Naturally.

Without the threat of punishment there is no joy in flight

In *The Woman in the Dunes* (1962), Kōbō Abe

In the desert there is no sign that says, Thou shalt not eat stones.

—SUFI PROVERB

In *The Handmaid's Tale* (1985), Margaret Atwood

Vengeance is mine, I will repay.

In *Anna Karenina* (serialized 1875–1877), Leo Tolstoy

Tolstoy's epigraph comes from the Bible, Romans 12:19. He explained his choice in a letter: "I selected it simply to express the idea that evil committed by man results in all bitter things that come from God and not from men, as Anna Karenina also experienced it..."

A man who has two women loses his soul.
But a man who has two houses loses his head.

In *A Perfect Spy* (1986), John le Carré

At the heart of this autobiographical novel is a fictionalized portrait of le Carré's father, Ronnie Cornwell, a renowned con artist. The novel's protagonist, Magnus Pym, concludes that being the son of a man with no conscience is better training for a spy than anything MI6 could provide. In real life, Ronnie Cornwell's scams ranged from bogus real estate deals to talking his way out of hotel bills. When he died in 1975, he had a fully staffed office at a fashionable London address, a country house, two racehorses, and not a dime to his name.

Nothing destroys a man more than being obligated to represent a country.

—JACQUES VACHÉ, LETTER
TO ANDRÉ BRETON

In *Hopscotch* (1963), Julio Cortázar

I was once more struck by the truth of the ancient saying: Man's heart is a ditch full of blood. The loved ones who have died throw themselves down on the bank of this ditch to drink the blood and so come to life again; the dearer they are to you, the more of your blood they drink.

—NIKOS KAZANTZAKIS, ZORBA THE GREEK

In *Day* (1961), Elie Wiesel

For want of a nail the shoe was lost.
For want of a shoe the horse was lost.
For want of a horse the rider was lost.
For want of a rider the battle was lost.
For want of a battle the kingdom was lost.
And all for the want of a horseshoe nail.

—TRADITIONAL

In *Started Early, Took My Dog* (2011), Kate Atkinson

Your ideas are terrifying and your hearts are faint. Your acts of pity and cruelty are absurd, committed with no calm, as if they were irresistible. Finally, you fear blood more and more. Blood and time.

—PAUL VALÉRY

In *Blood Meridian* (1985), Cormac McCarthy

A friend loveth at all times, and a brother is born for adversity.

—PROVERBS XVII, 17

In *The Mountain Lion* (1947), Jean Stafford

It would seem that both Jean Stafford and her brother Dick were born for adversity. By the time Stafford wrote *The Mountain Lion*, featuring a brother-sister pair modeled on the young Staffords, Dick would be dead, killed in World War II in an ambulance accident in France. A car accident also figures prominently in Jean's life. Her future husband, the poet Robert Lowell, drove a car into a wall, escaping unscathed, while Jean suffered severe facial injuries that led to the loss of her looks and her health. Her turbulent marriage to Lowell would end in divorce. She would eventually find happiness with her third husband, the writer A. J. Liebling.

To talk of diseases is a sort of *Arabian Nights* entertainment.

—WILLIAM OSLER

In *The Man Who Mistook His Wife for a Hat* (1985),
Oliver Sacks

Known as the "Father of Modern Medicine," William Osler (1849–1919) was one of the founders of Johns Hopkins Hospital and acclaimed as a clinician, humanitarian, and teacher. Insisting that medical students learn best from seeing and talking to patients, he was the first to bring them out of the lecture halls and into the wards, establishing the model of medical residency. His *Principles and Practice of Medicine*, published in 1892, was the first great textbook of modern medicine. Devastated by the death of his only son, a soldier killed on the Western Front, Osler died in the Spanish flu pandemic that followed in World War I's wake.

The Existential
Epigraph

———

We know the sound of two hands clapping.
But what is the sound of one hand clapping?

—A ZEN KOAN

In *Nine Stories* (1953), J. D. Salinger

Each man's destiny is personal only insofar as it may happen to resemble what is already in his memory.

—EDUARDO MALLEA

In *The Sheltering Sky* (1949), Paul Bowles

One day in 1928, Paul Bowles, a young composer and unhappy college freshman, sat in his dorm room and flipped a coin. Heads, he would drop out and go to Europe. Tails, he would commit suicide by overdosing on pills. Europe it was. In Berlin he met Christopher Isherwood, who named the heroine of the story he was writing, "Sally Bowles," after Paul. In France he met Gertrude Stein, who suggested he try Morocco. He shared a house in Tangier with composer Aaron Copland, who helped Bowles with his musical career. Back in New York in the mid-1930s, he met his soul mate, Jane Auer. Despite the fact that she was a lesbian and he was bisexual, they were married within a year. In 1947, Bowles decided to return to Tangier, where he wrote his fever dream of a novel, *The Sheltering Sky*. About the psychological dread that pervades the novel, Bowles has said: "If I stress various facets of unhappiness, it is because I believe unhappiness should be studied very carefully . . . You must watch your universe as it cracks above your head."

Each conscience seeks the death of the other.

—HEGEL

In *She Came to Stay* (1943), Simone de Beauvoir

I shall see an end of faith, nothing
To be beleeved that I doe not know . . .

—JOHN DONNE, from *A SERMON*
PREACHED AT A MARRIAGE, 30 MAY 1621

In *The Sun at Midday* (1997), Gini Alhadeff

For I tell you that God is able of these stones to raise up children to Abraham.

In *The Seven Storey Mountain* (1948), Thomas Merton

Merton's biblical epigraph is Matthew 3:9. The words are John the Baptist's as he addresses the hostile Pharisees and Sadducees and speaks of the imminent arrival of Jesus.

Men ask the way to Cold Mountain.
Cold Mountain: there's no through trail.

—HAN-SHAN

In *Cold Mountain* (1997), Charles Frazier

The ninth-century Chinese poet and hermit who adopted the name Han-Shan ("Cold Mountain") was born to privilege, but did not succeed in either civil or military service. Although not directly involved in an unsuccessful rebellion, Han-Shan was forced to flee for his life when the emperor returned to power. Anonymity was thus a practical choice for the poet, who sequestered himself in a remote region, writing his poems on rocks and temple walls. Two hundred years after Han-Shan's death, someone copied and collected the three hundred–plus poems which have come down to us. Jack Kerouac dedicated his novel *The Dharma Bums* to the wanderer known as Han-Shan.

He rests. He has traveled.

—JAMES JOYCE, ULYSSES

In *What I Lived For* (1994), Joyce Carol Oates

By homely gift and hindered Words
The human heart is told
Of Nothing—
"Nothing" is the force
That renovates the World—

—EMILY DICKINSON (#1563)

In *The Sweet Hereafter* (1991), Russell Banks

Probably just somebody's nasty black poodle. But I've always wondered . . . What if it really was Him, and He decided I wasn't worth it?

—TONY KUSHNER, *A BRIGHT ROOM CALLED DAY*

In *In the Woods* (2007), Tana French

* * *

God moves the player, he, in turn, the piece. But what god beyond God begins the round of dust and time and dream and agonies?

—JORGE LUIS BORGES

In *No Other Life* (1993), Brian Moore

'Tis all a chequer-board of Nights and Days
Where Destiny with Men for pieces plays:
Hither and thither moves, and mates, and
    slays,
And one by one back in the Closet lays.
                    —*THE RUBÁIYÁT OF OMAR KHAYYÁM*

In *Wolf to the Slaughter* (1967), Ruth Rendell

"I have really got a hold of an old Epicurean so desperately impious in his recommendation to live for Today . . . . he is very tender about his Roses and his Wine, and making the most of this poor little life." So wrote Edward FitzGerald to his friend Alfred, Lord Tennyson, about a Persian poem-cycle he was translating. Omar Khayyám was an eleventh-century mathematician and astronomer whose groundbreaking work was virtually unknown in the West. His *Rubáiyát* is a series of quatrains that FitzGerald published anonymously in 1859. Sales were worse than poor. However, in 1861, Dante Gabriel Rossetti spotted the book on a remainder table and bought it for a penny. The *Rubáiyát* was soon popular with Pre-Raphaelites and Victorian aesthetes, and its fame spread to America. It was not until 1870 that FitzGerald stepped forward as the man responsible for bringing Khayyám to English-speaking audiences. He would spend the rest of his life attempting to perfect his translation.

But who shall dwell in these worlds if they be inhabited? . . . Are we or they the Lords of the World? . . . And how are all things made for man?

—KEPLER, quoted in *THE ANATOMY OF MELANCHOLY*

In *The War of the Worlds* (1898), H. G. Wells

Q. What are the four last things to be ever remembered?
A. The four last things to be ever remembered are Death, Judgment, Hell, and Heaven.

—THE PENNY CATECHISM

In *Memento Mori* (1959), Muriel Spark

There is no steady unretracing progress in this life; we do not advance through fixed gradations, and at the last one pause: through infancy's unconscious spell, boyhood's thoughtless faith, and adolescence' doubt (the common doom), then skepticism, then disbelief, resting at last in manhood's pondering repose of If. But once gone through, we trace the round again; and are infants, boys, and men, and Ifs eternally. Where lies the final harbor, whence we unmoor no more?

—HERMAN MELVILLE, *MOBY-DICK*

In *Blind Faith* (1989), Joe McGinniss

I am the man, I suffered, I was there.

—WHITMAN

In *Giovanni's Room* (1956), James Baldwin

I am not I; thou art not he or she; they are not they.

—E.W.

In *Brideshead Revisited* (1945), Evelyn Waugh

In 1944, Captain Evelyn Waugh wrote to his commanding officer requesting a three-month leave of absence. The reason? A book he needed to write. "If, in fact, the book is not written now, it will never be written." Remarkably, leave was granted and Waugh returned in imagination to the summer of 1931 spent largely at Madresfield, the ancestral home of the Lygon family. He had been to Oxford with Hugh, the model for the novel's Sebastian Flyte, and became close to his sisters Maimie and Coote. With the novel complete, Waugh accompanied Randolph Churchill, the prime minister's son, on a mission to Croatia. Their plane crashed, killing ten of the nineteen people on board. Waugh was badly burned and sent to Bari, Italy, for treatment. Coote, in the Women's Auxiliary Air Force, was stationed nearby and visited regularly. He told her about the book and she registered his anxiety over publicizing her family's scandals. Waugh's disclaimer had limited success. His friend Nancy Mitford weighed in with a field report: "General view: It is the Lygon family."

For here have we no continuing city . . .

—SAINT PAUL

In *Ship of Fools* (1962), Katherine Anne Porter

Enigma and evasion grow;
And shall we never find Thee out?

—HERMAN MELVILLE, *CLAREL*

In *Damascus Gate* (1998), Robert Stone

UNEXPECTED
SOURCES

All seats provide equal viewing of the universe.
—MUSEUM GUIDE, HAYDEN PLANETARIUM

In *A Gate at the Stairs* (2009), Lorrie Moore

You will have the tallest, darkest leading man in Hollywood.

—MERIAN C. COOPER TO FAY WRAY

In *Gravity's Rainbow* (1973), Thomas Pynchon

The studio boss responsible for teaming Ginger Rogers and Fred Astaire, Cooper (1893–1973) was also director John Ford's favorite producer to work with. The idea for *King Kong* (1933) came to Cooper in a dream. He would co-write, co-direct, and appear in the film. In later years he would become a backer of Senator Joseph McCarthy's campaign to root out suspected Communists in Hollywood. His achievements in the film industry earned him a star on Hollywood's Walk of Fame, but his name is misspelled as "Meriam C. Cooper."

"Most of you, I am sure, remember the tragic circumstances of the death of Geoffrey Clifton at Gilf Kebir, followed later by the disappearance of his wife, Katharine Clifton, which took place during the 1939 desert expedition in search of Zerzura.

"I cannot begin this meeting tonight without referring very sympathetically to those tragic occurrences.

"The lecture this evening . . ."

—FROM THE MINUTES OF THE
GEOGRAPHICAL SOCIETY MEETING
OF NOVEMBER 194–, LONDON

In *The English Patient* (1992), Michael Ondaatje

YOU DESERVE THE BEST OF EVERYTHING

The best job, the best surroundings, the best pay, the best contacts.

—FROM AN AD IN *THE NEW YORK TIMES*

In *The Best of Everything* (1958), Rona Jaffe

Based on her experiences working in publishing in the 1950s, *The Best of Everything* was Jaffe's (1931–2005) first novel, a runaway best seller. Fifteen compulsively readable books followed. While Jaffe's heroines were often in search of the perfect husband, the author herself preferred to avoid "the rat race to the altar" and remained single. Success was not all diamonds and champagne for Jaffe. In 1995 she established the Rona Jaffe Foundation to "identify and support women writers of exceptional talent," bestowing annual writers' awards accompanied by generous financial grants. Past winners have included Rivka Galchen, ZZ Packer, and Elif Batuman.

Nothing is more priceless and more worthy of preservation than the rich array of animal life with which our country has been blessed. It is a many-faceted treasure, of value to scholars, scientists, and nature lovers alike, and it forms a vital part of the heritage we all share as Americans.

—PRESIDENT RICHARD NIXON, STATEMENT UPON SIGNING THE ENDANGERED SPECIES ACT OF 1973

In *100 Heartbeats: The Race to Save Earth's Most Endangered Species* (2009), Jeff Corwin

It's amazing I won. I was running against peace, prosperity, and incumbency.

—GEORGE W. BUSH, JUNE 14, 2001, SPEAKING TO SWEDISH PRIME MINISTER GÖRAN PERRSON, UNAWARE THAT A LIVE TELEVISION CAMERA WAS STILL ROLLING

In *Stupid White Men* (2002), Michael Moore

Of what import are brief, nameless lives . . . to Galactus??

—FANTASTIC FOUR, STAN LEE & JACK KIRBY (VOL. I, NO. 49, APRIL 1966)

In *The Brief Wondrous Life of Oscar Wao* (2007), Junot Díaz

At one time the earth was probably a white-hot sphere like the sun.

—TARR AND MCMURRY

In *Look Homeward, Angel* (1929), Thomas Wolfe

Wolfe's epigraph quotes the 1900 school textbook by geographer Ralph S. Tarr, who led an 1896 expedition to Greenland, and educator Frank M. McMurry.

In a knot of eight crossings, which is about the average-size knot, there are 256 different "over and under" arrangements possible. . . . Make only one change in this "over and under" sequence and either an entirely different knot is made or no knot at all may result.

—*THE ASHLEY BOOK OF KNOTS*

In *The Shipping News* (1993), Annie Proulx

I meant what I said, and I said what I
   meant . . .
An elephant's faithful—one hundred per cent!

—*THEODOR SEUSS GEISEL, HORTON
HATCHES THE EGG* (1940)

In *Water for Elephants* (2006), Sara Gruen

An oak is a tree. A rose is a flower. A deer is an animal. A sparrow is a bird. Russia is our fatherland. Death is inevitable.

—P. SMIRNOVSKI, *A TEXTBOOK OF RUSSIAN GRAMMAR*

In *The Gift* (1963), Vladimir Nabokov

ACKNOWLEDGMENTS

Thanks to Peter Borland and Judith Curr at Atria Books, whose excellent idea this book is—and for believing me to be the right bibliophile for the job. Production editor Loretta Denner and copy editor David Chesanow made this a better book through their dedication to facts and language and their rigorous-yet-gentle professionalism. I spent many happy hours collecting epigraphs in my favorite hunting grounds: Posman Books, Grand Central branch; Strand Book Store, New York City; Oblong Books in Millerton, New York; the Mercantile Library on East Forty-seventh Street; and the Roe-Jan Community Library in Hillsdale, New York. The printed word thrives and I'm grateful to all who stock, maintain, and staff these treasure houses. I'm indebted to Sharon Powers for help with French translations. More than gratitude goes to David Hunt, who has brought me all good things, including numerous dusty paperbacks.

INDEX

THE ORIGINAL SOURCES OF
THE EPIGRAPHS ARE:

ADDITIONAL SOURCES